ON

SPINOZA

Diane Steinberg
Cleveland State University

Wadsworth
Thomson Learning.

Australia • Canada • Mexico • Singapore • Spain
United Kingdom • United States

Printed in the United States of America
1 2 3 4 5 6 7 03 02 01 00 99

For permission to use material from this text, contact us:
Web: http://www.thomsonrights.com
Fax: 1-800-730-2215
Phone: 1-800-730-2214

For more information, contact:
Wadsworth/Thomson Learning, Inc.
10 Davis Drive
Belmont, CA 94002-3098
USA
http://www.wadsworth.com

ISBN: 0-534-57612-5

Contents

1

Introduction

Spinoza's philosophy is attractive and worth studying for many reasons, but perhaps the most important is that it offers a unified and deep view of all the issues which matter to us philosophically, such as the nature of reality, human nature, what we can know and the good life. There are three fundamental features of his philosophy which particularly contribute to its unity—the doctrine of substance monism, the unrelenting naturalism, and the geometric mode of exposition which Spinoza employs in the *Ethics*.

The doctrine of substance monism is the hallmark of Spinoza's philosophy. Spinoza was neither the first nor the last philosopher to espouse metaphysical monism, or the doctrine that reality is one. The first was Parmenides (*ca.* 500 B.C.E.) who maintained that what is (reality) is eternal, immutable, homogeneous, continuous, immobile, complete and whole, "like the bulk of a well-rounded sphere".[1] In the late nineteenth century the British Idealists conceived of reality as a single all-embracing experience (the absolute), within which all finite experiences were somehow subsumed.[2] Spinoza's monism is superior to both of these doctrines, but in different ways. Unlike Parmenides, Spinoza does not deny the reality of difference, but rather explains it. The contrast between Spinoza's monism and that of the British Idealists is more complex, but two points can be made briefly. First, unlike the British Idealists, Spinoza does not reduce or subordinate matter to mind—extension and thought are equally real in his philosophy. Second, in offering the principle of the unity of a single experience to explain the unity of reality, the British Idealists gave us little more than

1

a metaphor which raises more questions than it answers. What principles explain the unity of a single experience? Spinoza's doctrine of substance monism, however, provides a basis for his articulation of principles which explain the unity of reality.

Another less immediately evident but pervasive and unifying feature of Spinoza's philosophy is its thoroughgoing naturalism. Spinoza is committed to explaining and analyzing everything in natural terms. As one recent commentator aptly put it, Spinoza even naturalized theology. [3] Spinoza titled the first part of his *Ethics* "On God," and God is both the beginning and the end of his philosophy in the sense that He is the ultimate cause in terms of which everything must be understood, and the ultimate object that we seek to know and love. Yet his views on God and His relation to the world bear only a superficial resemblance to those of traditional monotheism. God is not a being who transcends nature, but God and the world are one, divine law is nothing but natural law, and God's power is identical with that of natural things. In his anthropology human beings are not distinguished from others by a transcendent purpose, by their free will, or even by their possession of a soul or mind. Nothing in nature has a transcendent purpose or end for which it exists. There are no final causes. Nothing acts by freedom of the will, but everything is determined by antecedent necessity. And everything is animate or besouled, although in different degrees (panpsychism). Animals are no more unfeeling machines than are humans, although their feelings differ from human feelings.

Spinoza's ethical doctrine is also completely naturalistic. Terms such as "good" and "beautiful" do not denote any real property of things but only how we are affected by them. We call things "good" because we desire them, not vice versa. Values originate from us, not from a transcendent source, and are relative to us. The only objective sense which can be given to "good" is that of being genuinely advantageous to human nature.

Perhaps the most obviously unifying—and at the same time most daunting—feature of Spinoza's philosophy is the geometrical form of exposition in which his major work, the *Ethics*, is cast. The *Ethics* contains a complete exposition of his entire mature philosophy and is written in the style of Euclid's *Elements*. In it Spinoza proceeds from explicitly stated definitions, axioms and postulates to propositions, which are demonstrated from the former along with previously demonstrated propositions. Commentators have offered a variety of reasons to explain why Spinoza chose the geometrical form to expound his philosophy. According to one the geometrical method of expositon was particularly suited to Spinoza's subject matter, with the logical relation of ground and consequent reflecting what he saw as the actual relation of cause and effect.[4] Another has suggested that he used it both for pedagogical reasons—to give a clear presentation to his students—and to conceal his ideas from hostile readers.[5] And according to yet another he used it because it was abstract, enabling him at once to suppress his own personality and avoid appeals to sense experience or emotion, and be the "mouthpiece" of reason itself.[6] My own view is that there are deeper and more compelling reasons why Spinoza chose the geometric method. One is that it is chiefly through seeing the interconnectedness of his entire philosophy that a reader can be convinced of its truth. Another is the practical value of a structured framework of thought. In any case, the exercise of putting his thought into the geometrical form had a unifying effect, fostering his aim of explaining all things in terms of a fairly small set of basic concepts and principles.

In the following account of Spinoza's philosophy I have tried to interpret his doctrines and his demonstrations in ways which show their strength and minimize internal conflicts. But Spinoza is not a "perfect" philosopher. There are well-known problems both with his substance monism and his attempt to maintain naturalism, as well as puzzles and inconsistencies at other points in his doctrine. And there are logical errors in many of his demonstrations. I have not focused on finding these flaws, but I have not tried to gloss over them either. Despite them, Spinoza seems to me to have achieved a degree of success in formulating a comprehensive and unified theoretical and practical philosophy which no other thinker has been able to match.

My exposition of Spinoza's philosophy is based primarily on the *Ethics*, since only this work contains his mature basic philosophical doctrines. With the exception of my final chapter, which deals with various aspects of his philosophical method, I have more or less followed the order in which topics are treated in the *Ethics*. My discussion of method comes last because Spinoza's methodology needs to be understood in terms of his substantive philosophy.

In many places I have presented Spinoza's doctrines against a (very roughly sketched) background of those of Descartes. This procedure is useful for understanding Spinoza for two reasons. One is that Descartes is probably Spinoza's most important philosophical predecessor. We know from his *Descartes' "Principles of Philosophy"* that Spinoza had an excellent and thorough understanding of Descartes, and that his views in fact developed against this background. The second is that in a vast number of its fundamental aspects Spinoza's philosophy is radically different from that of Descartes; viewing the two in contrast is highly illuminating and enhances the understanding of Spinoza.

*   *   *   *   *

Spinoza was born November 24, 1632, in Amsterdam.[7] His family were Spanish Jews who had emigrated, via Portugal to the Netherlands in the previous generation. In the Netherlands Jews enjoyed relative freedom from persecution; many, including Spinoza's father, were active in Dutch commerce. Spinoza was given a traditional Jewish education within the community. He grew up speaking Spanish and learning Hebrew. He learned Dutch as a result of living in Amsterdam, and in his early twenties mastered Latin. All of his philosophical works appear to have been originally written in Latin. The details of Spinoza's life reveal a man who lived in accordance with the values implied by his doctrines—knowledge, independence of mind, personal integrity, and a broad concern for one's fellow human beings.   Both his early biographers, J. M. Lucas and Colerus (Johann Kohler) praise his character, even though Colerus, a Lutheran minister, found his doctrines "impious and absurd."[8]

At the age of twenty-four Spinoza was officially "anathematized" or excommunicated by the elders of the Amsterdam Jewish community. This meant he was forbidden to associate with any Jews from then on, and they were likewise forbidden to associate with him or to read his writings. Why this event took place is a matter of some speculation. The official proclamation of excommunication referred to "the abominable heresies practiced and taught by him" and "other enormities committed by him" for which there were "many trustworthy witnesses."[9] J.M. Lucas, the only biographer of Spinoza who actually knew him, recounts how he was enticed by some false friends into admitting that he found nothing in the bible which was inconsistent with God's being corporeal, angels' being mere phantoms, and the soul's being nothing more than the principle of life. They then spread rumors about him and reported him to the authorities of the synagogue, who called him to appear before them "to give and account of his faith."[10]   At the hearing, the false friends testified

> that they had heard him scoff at the Jews as "superstitious
> people born and bred in ignorance, who do not know what
> God is, and who nevertheless have the audacity to speak of
> themselves as His people, to the disparagement of other
> nations. As for the Law, it was instituted by a man who was
> forsooth better versed than they were in the matter of Politics,
> but who was hardly more enlightened than they were in
> Physics or even in Theology; with an ounce of good sense one

could discover the imposture, and one must be as stupid as the Hebrews of the time of Moses to believe that gallant man."[11]

One explanation as to why Spinoza was deemed to have committed acts worthy of permanent excommunication is that the religious authorities, fearful of giving offence to the Dutch, were protecting the place of the Jews of Amsterdam within the larger community. On this way of looking at the matter, the excommunication of Spinoza was a way of dissociating the community from someone whose views were heretical and dangerous from the point of view of Christianity.[12] Yirmiyahu Yovel, howver, points out that at the time of Spinoza's excommunication, the position of the Jews in Amsterdam was relatively secure. Yovel's explanation is that, faced with the continuous task of integrating new Marrano arrivals into Jewish culture, the leaders of the Amsterdam Jewish community saw Spinoza's views and actions as a threat to the survival of the community because they tended to undermine the authority of religious and cultural tradition.[13] Lucas' report of the testimony given against Spinoza (above) tends to support this explanation..

Although philosophy was the main work of Spinoza's life, he learned the craft of lens-grinding by which he partly supported himself. While this activity probably contributed to his early death, it also provided a connection with some of the leading scientific figures of the day, such as Huygens. For his subsistence he had in addition a small annuity left to him by a friend and disciple who died at an early age, Simon DeVries. But he declined offers of greater support from DeVries, and later, an offer of a pension from the King of France in return for the dedication of a work to him. He also declined an offer of a professorship at the University of Heidelberg, partly bcause he feared that teaching duties would interfere with his efforts to develop his philosophy, and also because it came with the expectation that he would not "disturb the publicly established religion" (letter 47).[14] In his words

> I do not know within what limits the freedom to philosophise must be confined if I am to avoid appearing to disturb the publicly established religion (letter 48).

In 1960 he left Amsterdam and moved to the village of Rijnsburg, near Leyden, in order to have peace and solitude in which to write. While at Rijnsburg he is thought to have written the (unfinished) *Treatise on the Emendation of the Understanding*, the *Short Treatise on God, Man and His Well-Being, Descartes' "Principles of Philosophy,* and a draft of at least the first part of his major work, the *Ethics.* The work on the philosophy of Descartes was begun with the aim of instructing a private pupil, but at the instigation of friends, was expanded and published in 1663. It is his only work to be published under his name in his lifetime.

In 1663 he moved again, to Voorburg, near the Hague. Here he was introduced to Jan DeWitt, the Grand Pensionary of Holland. By June, 1665, a draft of what was to become parts III and IV of the *Ethics* was nearly completed. But, evidently stimulated by current political events and his proximity to them, Spinoza laid it aside to work on his *Theologico-Political Treatise*. The Dutch Republic, whose center of government was the Hague, was a loose federation of seven provinces, of which the richest and most influential was Holland. DeWitt stood for religious toleration and freedom of expression; he was opposed by the Calvinist clergy and others who wanted to establish a state religion, who supported the Prince of Orange. The struggle between the two camps was complicated by setbacks in the war with England and Sweden (1665-1667), and later the war with England and France (1672). Spinoza became a friend and supporter of DeWitt. In correspondence Spinoza declared that his aim in writing the *Theologico-Political Treatise* was to expose the prejudices of theologians, vindicate himself against the charge of atheism, and defend the freedom of philosophizing and saying what one thinks (letter 30). When he published it in 1670, the situation was dangerous enough that he had to do so anonymously, even though its publication was under the protection of DeWitt.

In 1670 Spinoza moved to the Hague and resumed work on the *Ethics*. Two years later, with a French army of over a hundred thousand men invading the Netherlands, the people looked to the Prince of Orange to save the country, casting blame on the DeWitts for the unpreparedness of the Dutch. While Jan DeWitt was visiting his brother Cornelius, imprisoned at the Hague, a mob broke in and brutally murdered both brothers. When Spinoza heard this news he was—uncharacteristically—overcome with emotion. (Lucas reports that he shed tears.[15]) He wrote a placard denouncing the act which he intended to post at the scene. His landlord, however, discerned the danger and locked him inside, thus preventing him from meeting a similar fate from the mob.

In the last few years of his life Spinoza finished his *Ethics* and worked on a political treatise and a Hebrew grammar. When the mere rumor of the impending publication of the *Ethics* stirred up controversy, he postponed it indefinitely. He died February 21, 1677, of consumption, from which he had suffered for many years. Following his death the *Ethics* was published in the *Opera Postuma*, along with the *Treatise on the Emendation of the Understanding*

6

(unfinished), the *Political Treatise* (unfinished), the *Hebrew Grammar* (unfinished), and some of his correspondence.

Endnotes

[1] Parmenides, Fragment 8, l. 43.

[2] A. E. Taylor's *Elements of Metaphysics*, Book II, provides a highly readable exposition of this version of metaphysical monism.

[3] Donagan 1988, 32 - 34. Donagan was the first commentator to stress Spinoza's naturalism.

[4] Joachim, 12 – 13.

[5] Wolfson, I, 22 – 24, 53 – 59.

[6] Hampshire, 25.

[7] My account of Spinoza's life draws on the early biographies of Colerus and Lucas, Spinoza's own correspondence, and the extensive biographical sketches presented in Pollock and Wolf 1910.

[8] Colerus, 432.

[9] As reported in Pollock, 18.

[10] Wolf 1927, 44 – 48. Jean Maximilian Lucas is believed to be the anonymous author of *The Life of the Late Mr. De Spinoza*, translated by A. Wolf in his *Oldest Biography of Spinoza*.

[11] Wolf 1927, 48 – 49.

[12] Pollock, 16.

[13] Yovel 1989, 12-13.

[14] References to Spinoza's correspondence will be given in the text. All quotations from the correspondence are from *The Letters*, trans. Samuel Shirley.

[15] Wolf 1927, 65.

2

Basic Metaphysics

The Historical Roots of Spinoza's Notion of Substance

For Spinoza, everything that is real falls into one of two basic categories, substance or mode. Substance is defined as "what is in inself and is conceived through itself, i.e., that whose concept does not require the concept of another thing, from which it must be formed" (I dfn3); mode as "the affections of a substance, *or* that which is in another through which it is also conceived" (Idfn5).[1] These two categories are meant to be exclusive and exhaustive of what there is. Something cannot be both in itself and in another; and everything must be either in itself or in another (Iax1). Spinoza's distinction between substance and mode has generally been taken to be that between a thing or subject and its properties or states (although we shall consider another interpretation below, pp. 23 - 28).

The concept of substance ultimately traces back to Aristotle, who wrote in the *Categories* that

> Substance, in the truest and primary and most definite sense of the word, is that which is neither predicable of a subject nor present in a subject; for instance, the individual man or horse.[2]

Aristotle's conception of substance emerges from an analysis partly based on grammar, in which the basic divisions are between individuals (Socrates, Trigger) , properties of individuals or "accidents" (short, tan), and kinds of individuals or properties (animal, horse, color). Properties or accidents must exist in an individual subject; i.e.,

8

there cannot be shortness apart from an individual that is short. Kinds of things ultimately require individuals of which they are predicted, i.e., animal is predicated of horse, but horse is predicated of individual horses (Trigger). Individual things such as Socrates and Trigger do not exist in a subject and are not predicated of anything. We do not say, for example, that "Horse is a Trigger." Aristotle appears to conclude from these asymmetries that primary substances are the most basic of everything that exists. He points out that "if [primary substances] . . . did not exist, it would be impossible for anything else to exist" and "primary substances are most properly called substances in virtue of the fact that they are the entities which underlie everything else, and that everything else is either predicated of them or present in them".[3] One might object to this by pointing out that there cannot be propertyless subjects any more than there can be subjectless properties—Socrates (a subject) must be running or walking or standing or sitting or reclining, etc. Aristotle may have been influenced by the asymmetry of grammatical form which does not allow terms denoting individuals to occupy a predicative position. ("Socrates" can only be a grammatical subject.) The asymmetry of grammar, however, does not show that there is an asymmetry in the existential dependence relation of subject and properties.

Aristotle went on to state, however, that

> The most distinctive mark of substance appears to be that, while remaining numerically one and the same, it is capable of admitting contrary qualities.[4]

A substance is that which can (and does) remain the same identical thing through change. If the color of Socrates' face changes because he remains a long time in the sun, then the original color (white) ceases to exist, and a new color (tan) takes its place. But Socrates remains the same individual throughout the change. Aristotle's primary substances then, may be viewed as more basic than their properties and as underlying them in the sense that as the subjects in which the properties exist, they persist through change of properties.

The notion of substance as a subject in which properties must exist is also expressed by Spinoza's immediate predecessor Descartes, when he writes that the term "substance"

> applies to everything in which whatever we perceive immediately resides, as in a subject, or to every thing by means of which whatever we perceive exists. By 'whatever we perceive' is meant any property, quality or attribute of which we have a real idea. The only idea we have of a substance itself, in the strict sense, is that it is the thing in which whatever we perceive . . . exists. . . .[5]

In his *Principles of Philosophy*, however, Descartes distinguished two notions of substance. The first construes substance as "a thing which exists in such a way as to depend on no other thing for its existence."[6] By this definition God is the only substance. But in another sense of the term, namely "things that need only the concurrence of God in order to exist" Descartes tells us that corporeal substance and mind (created thinking substance) are substances.[7]

Although the notion of substance as a subject of properties and predication is common to Descartes and Aristotle, Descartes' additional criterion of independent existence significantly restricts what can count as a substance even when that condition is weakened to allow for substances which depend the concurrence of God alone. Individual bodies, such as that of a human being or horse, easily and inevitably suffer destruction from natural causes, hence fail to qualify as created substance. Only body "in general" or matter taken as a whole is properly considered a substance. The mind or soul, however, which on Descartes' view is a thing entirely distinct from body, is a substance, i.e., a thing which is incorruptible by nature and unable to cease to exist unless God denies it his concurrence.[8]

Spinoza's definition of substance as that which is in itself and is conceived through itself, taken in conjunction with the definition of mode as "that which is in another through which it is also conceived" suggests that he too thinks of substance as the subject in which properties (modes) must exist, and as a thing whose existence is independent of other things.[9] But whereas Aristotle took the term to apply to ordinary individuals such as men and horses, and Descartes took it to apply (in not the same but in related senses) to God, matter as a whole and created minds, Spinoza adopted the radical position that there is only one substance, namely God, or "substance consisting of an infinity of attributes," and consequently, that everything else must be a mode of, or *in*, the one substance or God. According to Spinoza what Descartes held to be the principal attributes (unvarying essential properties) of the two fundamental types of created substance— extension and thought—are properly understood as attributes of the one absolutely infinite substance; and individual minds and bodies (Aristotle's primary substances--horses and men) are properly understood as modes of that one substance.

Spinoza's basic doctrine of substance is developed in the first fourteen propositions of *Ethics* I, which culminate in the demonstration that

> Except God, no substance can be or be conceived (Ip14).

We can begin to understand Spinoza's substance by tracing the route by which he reaches this startling conclusion.

Spinoza's Argument for Substance Monism

In outline Spinoza's argument that there is only one substance—absolutely infinite substance or God—appears straightforward and simple (Ip14dem). It is as follows:

1. There cannot be two substances of the same attribute (Ip5).
2. God is a substance consisting of an infinity of attributes (Idfn6).
3. God necessarily exists (Ip11).
4. Any substance other than God would have to have some attribute in common with God (from 2).

Conclusion: No substance besides God can exist or be conceived (Ip14).[10]

We shall examine the reasoning behind each premise of Spinoza's argument.

Premise 1

Clearly the notion of "attribute" is a key one here. Spinoza defines an attribute as "what the intellect perceives of a substance, as constituting its essence" (Idfn4). He thinks it follows from this definition along with that of substance ("what is in itself and is conceived through itself"—Idfn3) that "Each attribute of a substance must be conceived through itself" (Ip10). It appears then that what Spinoza means by an attribute is very like what Descartes means by his notion of a principal attribute, which he elaborated as follows:

> A substance may indeed be known through any attribute at all; but each substance has one principal property which constitutes its nature and essence, and to which all its other properties are referred. Thus extension in length, breadth and depth constitutes the nature of corporeal substance; and thought constitutes the nature of thinking substance. Everything else which can be attributed to body presupposes extension, and is merely a mode of an extended thing; and similarly, whatever we find in the mind is simply one of the various modes of thinking. For example, shape is unintelligible except in an extended thing. . . ; while imagination, sensation and will are intelligible only in a thinking thing. By contrast, it is possible to understand extension without shape. . . and thought without imagination

or sensation . . . .[11]

So Spinoza is in agreement with Descartes insofar as he thinks of attributes as conceptually basic, essential features of substance, and even with respect to what known attributes of substance there are, namely extension and thought. He disagrees with Descartes, however, in holding that no two substances can have the same attribute (Ip5). For Descartes, all finite minds share the principle attribute of thought.

Spinoza's reasoning for Ip5 rests partly on Ip4, that

> Two or more distinct things are distinguished from one another, either   by a difference in the attributes of the substances or by a difference in their affections.

This propoosition is Spinoza's version of a metaphysical principle (made famous by Leibniz) known as the Identity of Indiscernables. In more familiar terminology it says that any numerically distinct things must have some qualitative difference, or there cannot be two (numerically distinct) things which have all the same qualitites. This is a controversial issue in philosophy, and Spinoza's Ip4 merely expresses this principle in his own terms, rather than proves it. In his system the only real qualitative differences are differences of the attributes, or differences of the affections (modes), of substance.

Applied to substance, Ip4 says: if there are two (or more) numerically distinct substances, they must have different attributes or different affections. For example, two substances could differ in one's being extended and the other's being thinking; or they might both be extended and differ in one's having a cubic shape, and the other having a spherical shape. But according to Ip4 they must—if they are two— differ in one of these ways. With Ip5, however, Spinoza is claiming that two numerically distinct substances cannot differ merely in their affections and not in their attributes; that is, there cannot be two numerically distinct extended substances, one of which is a cube and the other a sphere. He argues that if there is merely a difference in the affections of substance, then

> since a substance is prior in nature to its affections (by P1), if the affections are put to one side and [the substance] is considered in itself, i.e., (by D3 and A6), considered truly, one cannot be conceived to be distinguished from another, i. e., (by P4), there cannot be many, but only one [of the same nature or attribute], q.e.d. (Ip5dem)

One might think Spinoza is begging the question here, or assuming the very point he wishes to prove. Why assume the affections can be put to one side?[12] What he has in mind, I think is something like this. Consider two bodies, A, which is red all over, and

B, which is blue all over. This qualitative difference is not what makes A and B two different things; rather it is because A and B are two different things that they can differ in overall color. So, to explain why A and B are two different things (that is, to say what makes them two) we need to find some more fundamental property in which they differ. Suppose it is their location in space. (We know no two bodies can be in the same place.) Again, being in different locations doesn't seem to explain why A and B are different; rather it is because they are different that they are able to be at different locations.

Perhaps the problem is that we are looking for the properties which make A and B distinct among the wrong type of properties. Color and location are what might be called nonessential properties, that is, properties which a thing can lose without itself going out of existence (which includes becoming a different thing). An essential property is one which a thing cannot lose without going out of existence. Clearly a body can lose its color (a red body can become blue) or change its location without going out of existence. What is essential to a body? Properties such as being extended, having some shape and size (but not any particular shape or size), some color, and so on. But these qualities are ones which A and B and all bodies share in common. Hence these essential properties are not properties which make one body different from another. At this point we might be inclined to say that A's being numerically different from B is just a matter of brute fact, not something which can be explained by their differing in some qualitative way. But if we do this we are simply taking a different position than Spinoza appears to be taking in Ip4,5, and their demonstrations. We are denying, while Spinoza is assuming, that numerical difference must be explained by qualitative difference. His conclusion would be that if you strip away all the nonessential properties of two bodies, and you leave only what is necessary for them (as bodies) to remain in existence, what is left is only undifferentiated body. This is so because there is nothing left which could differentiate one body from another. To connect this with Spinoza's demonstration of Ip5, recall that an attribute is what constitutes the essence of substance. A substance can change its modes without going out of existence; hence no particular mode is essential to a substance. Thus, when Spinoza is considering what distinguishes one substance from another it is reasonable for him to "put aside" the modifications of substance and consider only its attributes. And since he assumes (Ip4) that any numerical distinction must be based on a qualitative distinction, it follows that there cannot be two substances of the same nature or attribute.

Premise 2

    The second premise of the argument is based on the definition of God (Idfn6), and consequently, might seem invulnerable to objection. Writers have different intentions, however, in setting forth definitions. Sometimes a writer merely intends to specify how she will use a term, or the meaning the term will have in her discussion. At other times a writer intends to assert what she takes to be the necessary and sufficient properties of a thing. The former is called a stipulative definition; the latter a real definition.

    Simon DeVries, who was both a friend and student of Spinoza, wrote to him on behalf of a group engaged in studying an early draft of the *Ethics*, requesting him to explain his views on the nature of definition. Spinoza responded:

> There is the definition that serves to explicate a thing whose essence alone is in question and the subject of doubt, and there is the definition which is put forward simply for examination. The former, since it has a determinate object, must be a true definition, while this need not be so in the latter case. . . . [A] definition either explicates a thing as it exists outside the intellect—and then it should be a true definition. . . --or it explicates a thing as it is conceived by us, or can be conceived. And in that case . . . [it is required] merely that it be conceived, not conceived as true. . . . So then a bad definition is one which is not conceived (letter 9).

Borrowing an example cited by DeVries to illustrate a bad definition of the latter sort, Spinoza added that if someone says that "two straight lines enclosing an area are to be called figurals" then "if by a straight line he means what we all mean, the thing is plainly inconceivable, and so there is no definition."

    In this passage it appears that Spinoza recognized two types of definition, coinciding with what we have called real and stipulative definitions, and that he held the former should be true, but the latter need only be logically consistent or conceivable. Given that Spinoza's letter was intended to address difficulties encountered by a group of persons studying his work, it is somewhat surprising that he does not say of which type his own definitions are intended to be. And, unfortunately, although he addresses the topic of definition elsewhere, nowhere does he explicitly say that the definitions with which he starts are either real or stipulative. Commentators have been divided as regards the question of how to take Spinoza's definitions in the *Ethics*. But it seems clear that we must take them as being put forth as real, thus subject to evaluation as true or false, since otherwise the *Ethics* would be a mere logical exercise and not a demonstation of the nature of things.[13]

From the standpoint of Cartesianism, there was an objection to his definition of God, which would apply even if that definition were offered merely as stipulative. Recall that according to Descartes, every substance has only one principal attribute which "constitutes its nature and essence." The reason why a substance can have only one such attribute is that such attributes are able to be conceived or understood by us entirely independently of one another. Therefore, since God can create things to be in whatever way we are able to conceive them, it follows that substances with different principal attributes are able to exist separately; and whenever two things can exist separately they are separate things.[14]

It is not surprising then that in the same letter in which he requested Spinoza's views on definition, DeVries wrote "you seem, Sir, to suppose that the nature of substance is so constituted that it can have several attributes, which you have not yet proved . . ." (letter 8). With this remark he called into question the conceivability of the definition of God as "substance consisting of an infinity of attributes, each of which expresses an eternal and infinite essence."

In his response to DeVries Spinoza claimed to have given two proofs that a substance can have more than one attribute:

> [T]he first . . . is as follows: It is clear beyond all doubt that every entity is conceived by us under some attribute, and the more reality or being an entity has, the more attributes are to be attributed to it. Hence an absolutely infinite entity must be defined. . . . A second proof—and this proof I take to be decisive—states that the more attributes I attribute to any entity, the more existence I am bound to attribute to it; that is, the more I conceive as truly existent. The exact contrary would be the case if I had imagined a chimera or something of that sort (letter 9).

What Spinoza here calls the first proof appears in the *Ethics* as Ip9 that "The more reality or being each thing has, the more attributes belong to it." In its demonstration Spinoza merely cites the definition of attribute (Idfn4). A line of thought similar to that involved in the second proof appears in the *Ethics* in Spinoza's third and fourth proofs for the existence of God (Ip11sch), which are discussed below. As proofs of the point at issue—whether or not the nature of substance is such that it can have more than one attribute—both points seem to beg the question.

Clearly Spinoza held a conception of the relation between substance and its essential attributes which was different from that of

Descartes, and he acknowledged this difference when he wrote in the scholium to Ip10 that

> From these propositions it is evident that although two attributes may be conceived to be really distinct (i.e., one may be conceived without the aid of the other), we still can not infer from that that they constitute two beings, *or* two different substances. For it is of the nature of a substance that each of its attributes is conceived through itself, since all the attributes it has have always been in it together, and one could not be produced by another, but each expresses the reality or being of substance (Ip10sch).

Thus, although Spinoza agrees with Descartes that the attributes of substance are conceived independently of one another, he explicitly rejects the latter's reasoning to the conclusion that they therefore constitute the essences of distinct substances. I shall return to the important question of how Spinoza understands the relation between substance and its attributes below, in the final section of chapter 3. For now we shall simply accept the logical consistency, or as Spinoza would say, the conceivability of the definition of God.

We shall also not raise any question regarding the truth of Spinoza's definition of God, but a few things need to be said about what it means. The full definition is

> By God I understand a being absolutely infinite, i.e., a substance consisting of an infinity of attributes, of which each one expresses an eternal and infinite essence.
>
> Exp.: I say absolutely infinite, not infinite in its own kind, for if something is only infinite in its own kind, we can deny infinite attributes of it . . . but if something is absolutely infinite, whatever expresses essence and involves no negation pertains to its essence (Idfn6).

Recall that an attribute is a conceptually basic, essential property of substance. When Spinoza says that God is "substance consisting of an infinity of attributes" he need not be taken to mean that God has an actually infinite number of such conceptually basic essential properties, but rather that He has all possible attributes. ("Infinite" means "not bounded" or "not limited.") As we have already mentioned, Spinoza agrees with Descartes that extension and thought are attributes of substance. Spinoza nowhere mentions any other attributes, and although he seems to leave open the possibility that there may be more, it is consistent with the definition of God that extension and thought be the only attributes.

Each of God's attributes "expresses an eternal and infinite

essence" or is infinite (unlimited) in its own kind. There is, in other words, nothing extended outside of God's attribute of extension which limits extension, and nothing outside of God's attribute of thought which limits His thought. In *Ethics* II Spinoza demonstrates that thought and extension are attributes of God from the fact of their (intellectually) perceived infinity or unlimitedness in their own kind (IIp1sch, 2dem). Since God consists of all possible unlimited-in-their-own-kind essences, He is absolutely infinite.

Finally, since God consists of all possible attributes, it follows that any other substance would have to have some attribute in common with God (step 4 of the argument).

Premise 3

Spinoza offers four separate proofs (three in the demonstration, one in the scholium) for Ip11, that "God, or a substance consisting of infinite attributes, each of which expresses eternal and infinite essence, necessarily exists." We shall focus our discussion here on the third and fourth because, for a number of reasons, neither the first nor the second appears to be a satisfactory demonstration that an absolutely infinite substance exists.

In the history of philosophy we can distinguish two basic types of argument for the existence of God. One is *a priori*, or based entirely on our understanding of concepts, of which the concept of God is the most crucial. The other is *a posteriori* or empirical—based at least partly on some fact or facts known through experience. Examples of the latter kind include the argument from design, which is based on the premise that the world and things in it are like an intricate machine with the parts fashioned and put together in a way to serve particular functions in the whole; and Descartes' argument for the existence of God in *Meditation* III which relies on the premise that he experiences within himself an idea of a perfect being.[15] The foremost example of an *a priori* proof for God's existence is Anselm's famous ontological argument in which he argues that from the mere concept of God as "something than which nothing greater can be thought," it follows that God must exist, since to suppose that such a being does not exist involves a contradiction.[16] The notion of "necessary existence" or of a being which "exists necessarily" or "whose essence involves existence" is closely related to the *a priori* form of argumentation. It is because it is believed to be possible to reason merely from the concept of God— what God is, or His essence—to the conclusion that He exists, that God is said to exist necessarily or that His essence is said to involve existence. Thus Spinoza lays it down as an axiom that "If a thing can be conceived as not existing, its essence does not involve existence" (Iax7), or less cumbersomely, "If the essence of a thing involves existence, then it must be conceived as existing."

Spinoza's fourth proof for God's existence is an *a priori* proof:

> [S]ince being able to exist is power, it follows that the more reality belongs to the nature of a thing, the more powers it has, of itself, to exist. Therefore, an absolutely infinite Being, *or* God, has, of himself, an absolutely infinite power of existing. For that reason, he exists absolutely (Ip11sch).

This argument explicitly states a principle on which the inference, from the concept of God to the fact that He exists, is supposed to rest. That principle is that the more reality a thing has, the more powers it has to exist. Unfortunately it is not obvious to a modern reader, even granting that God's nature is such that He has an absolutely infinite power of existing, how or that it follows that God in fact exists. Possibly Spinoza has in mind that it would be contradictory to suppose that a being with an absolutely infinite power of existing did not exist since that would be to suppose that there could be some limitation on its power to exist. In his third proof, however, Spinoza offers a slightly different line of reasoning based on the same principle. There he argues that since ability to exist is power, then, granting that we ourselves exist, if only finite beings exist, finite beings are more powerful (at least with respect to their capacity to exist) than an absolutely infinite being. Spinoza downplays this argument because it rests on the *a posteriori* claim that we ourselves exist; but it has the virtue of showing exactly how the advance is made from the concept of God as having absolutely infinite power to the conclusion that God exists.

The advantage and importance of both these arguments can be seen by contrasting them briefly with the first. In that argument Spinoza reasons from Ip7 that "It pertains to the nature of substance to exist," to the conclusion that an absolutely infinite substance must exist. Clearly if this reasoning works, it works equally for any conceivable substance. If Spinoza had no other argument for the existence of God or substance consisting of an infinity of attributes, then the most he could conclude from the additional premise that no two substances can share the same nature or attribute (Ip5) would be that either God exists and no other substance exists or that a plurality of substances (all having different attributes) exists and God does not exist. The principle on which Spinoza's third and fourth arguments for Ip11 rests, however, provides a means of arguing that the second alternative is impossible. If what exists were only a plurality of substances each only infinite in its own kind (substances possessing only a finite number of attributes), then such substances would be more powerful than an absolutely infinite substance, which contradicts the principle that "the more reality a thing has, the more powers it has, of itself, to exist."

Granted that God is the only substance, then since whatever exists is either a substance or a mode of substance, and since modes must exist in substance, it follows that "Whatever is, is in God, and nothing can be or be conceived without God" (Ip15).

The Development of Substance Monism

If the one substance doctrine is to have any meaning and interest as a metaphysical monism (as a claim that reality is one) it must do two things. First, it must recognize the diversity of reality; second it must explain in a non-trivial way how the diverse elements of reality are united into a single whole. In other words, diversity must not be explained away as mere illusion; and the whole must be more than a mere aggregate. Spinoza's system admits two kinds of diversity, that of the attributes of substance (diversity of kinds of thing) and that of its modes (diversity of things within a kind).[17] In the remainder of this chapter I shall first discuss how the multiplicity of the attributes of substance presents a serious and fundamental challenge to understanding the unity of substance. I shall then discuss how Spinoza's conception of the relation of substance and mode secures the unity of modes of a single attribute. At the end of chapter 3 I shall return to the problem of the unity of the attributes in a single substance.

Substance "Consisting of Infinite Attributes"

The attributes are conceptually independent, essential features of substance, which are general in the sense that the modes of substance must all be conceived or understood in terms of an attribute. A rock, for example, must be conceived as extended, and a mind must be conceived as thinking. Since the attributes are conceptually independent of one another, they are also causally independent—none is the cause or effect of any other. (Conceptual independence implies causal independence according to Spinoza, because knowledge of an effect involves knowledge of its cause—Iax4.) Thus, for Spinoza to hold that the one substance consists of a multiplicity of attributes is for him to hold that reality consists of fundamentally diverse kinds of things—extended things, thinking things, and whatever other fundamental types of thing there may be. He needs to explain how these diverse kinds of thing constitute a single reality, or what is the same thing, how the attributes are united in a single substance.

One natural way to attempt to explain the unity of the attributes is to think of them as being "in" substance, as properties are in a subject. Although this appears to be how Descartes (at least sometimes) thinks of the relation between a substance and its principal attribute, it is not how Spinoza thinks of the relation of substance and its attributes.[18] For Spinoza, what is "in" substance is a mode. We have already seen, however, that in Spinoza's system everything real is either a substance or a mode. Hence, if an attribute is not a mode, then assuming it is something real, it must—at least in some sense—be identical with substance. And in fact the definition of attribute as "what the intellect perceives of a substance, as constituting its essence," seems to indicate an identity between substance and attribute—a thing and its essence are not two things.

In Idfn6 as well as other passages in *Ethics* I Spinoza appears to identify God or absolutely infinite substance with the totality of the attributes (Ip19; 20cor2; 29sch.). But if God is the totality of his attributes, and each of the attributes is absolutely independent of every other, what makes this totality *one*? Another way of putting the problem is: how does a single substance consisting of an infinity of attributes, each of which expresses eternal and infinite essence, differ from an infinity of substances of one attribute, each of which is infinite in its own kind? God's essence appears to be irreducibly plural. (Obviously this problem is not solved by taking extension and thought to be the only attributes, since two is still a multiplicity, and reality is bifurcated into two distinct and independent realms.).

The problem of the unity of the attributes in a single substance reappears at the level of modes in the following way. What unites the diverse modes is that they are all modes of the one substance. But a mode is always a mode of an attribute of the one substance, or a mode of the one substance conceived under an attribute (Ip14cor2; 25cor). Thus, bodies are modes of extension (IIdfn1); and minds are modes of thought. It would seem then that to explain the unity of modes of different attributes, it is necessary to explain the unity of the attributes. As we shall see in the next chapter, however, Spinoza seems to solve the problem by working backwards. That is, his answer to the question of how the plurality of attributes can constitute the essence of a single substance emerges from his articulation of the relationship between modes of different attributes.

Substance and Its Modes: Two Interpretations

Turning now to Spinoza's treatment of modal diversity within a single attribute, here we can say, without intrusion of the diversity of attributes, that what unites distinct modes is that they are modes of, or *in*, the one substance or God. We may well ask, however, what it means for modes to be *in* substance or God. In the remaining part of *Ethics* I (p15 - p34) Spinoza turns to explaining the relation between the one substance, God, and everything else. The main focus of his treatment is how God causes the world. I shall give a brief description of Spinoza's very abstract account. Then, in order to make it less abstract, I shall present two recent interpretations of the relation of extended substance to bodies (modes of extension).

Because everything other than God is in God Spinoza rejects the traditional conception of a creator distinct from its creation; thus, "God is the immanent, not the transitive, cause of all things" (Ip18). Spinoza distinguishes within the one substance or God between what he calls n*atura naturans* ("nature naturing"), by which he means

> what is in itself and is conceived through itself, *or* such attributes of substance as express an eternal and infinite essence, i.e., (by P14C1 and P17C2), God, insofar as he is considered as a free cause (Ip29sch);

and *natura naturata* ("nature natured"), which he explains as

> whatever follows from the necessity of God's nature, *or* from any of   God's attributes, i.e., all the modes of God's attributes insofar as they are considered as things which are in God, and can neither be nor be conceived without God.

Spinoza holds that God is omnipotent insofar as every mode which can be conceived through any attribute must follow from that attribute or be produced by God (Ip16, 17cor2sch). And God alone is free in the sense that "God acts from the laws of his nature alone, and is compelled by no one" (Ip17).   But he is not omnipotent or free in the sense of these terms which entails being able to do or forebear a thing according to an undetermined will (Ip32, 32cor1,2). Everything which follows from God's nature—both finite and infinite modes—is strictly determined by God, as is summed up in Ip29: "In nature there is nothing contingent, but all things have been determined from the necessity of the divine nature to exist and produce an effect in a certain way" (see also Ip25, 26, 27, and 33).

Within *natura naturata* (what is in God and follows from or is produced by his attributes) Spinoza distinguishes two chains of causation. The first describes a series of things which follow "from the absolute nature" of (or, we might say, directly from) an attribute of God. Since the attributes are eternal (exist necessarily, Ip19) and infinite (unlimited by anything of the same kind), whatever follows from their absolute nature must itself be eternal and infinite; and whatever follows from a mode which follows directly from an attribute will itself be eternal and infinite (Ip21,22). In the *Ethics* Spinoza does not say what these infinite modes are, but elsewhere he identifies the immediate and mediate infinite modes of extension as motion and rest, and the face of the whole universe; and the immediate infinite mode of thought as absolutely infinite intellect (letter 64).

Since whatever is produced by the absolute nature of an attribute of God or by a modification which is infinite and always exists must itself be infinite and always exist (Ip23), it follows that the causal chain which begins with the absolute nature of an attribute will never descend to finite things. What is infinite and always exists can only give rise to what is infinite and always exists. Finite things can be produced only by "an attribute of God insofar as it is modified by a modification which is finite and has a determinate existence" (Ip28dem). Thus, since every finite thing requires a prior finite cause, the chain of finite causality extends backwards *ad infinitum* (Ip28). Exactly how the two causal chains are connected and what causal connection there is supposed to be between God's essence (the attributes) and finite modes, is not precisely spelled out.

In my discussion of the ancestry of Spinoza's notion of substance (above, pp. 8 – 10) I pointed out that for both Aristotle and Descartes the concept of substance involved being a subject of properties or (in grammatical terms) predication, and I suggested that Spinoza's notion of substance also involved this. E. M. Curley, however, thinks that Spinoza did not intend the relation between substance and mode to be understood as that of a subject to its properties. One reason is that modes are individual things (horses, humans), but these are of the "wrong logical type" to be predicated of a subject.[19] He admits that one might give a sense to saying that one thing (e.g., an individual human being) is a property of another (God). The most obvious meaning to attach to this is that to say one thing is a property of another thing is to say all the properties of the first are properties of the second. But this has at best unacceptable consequences—if a person is sinful, then God is sinful, etc.[20]

According to Curley, the relation of substance and mode is purely that of a cause to its effects.[21] That is, Spinoza's concept of substance as that which is in itself and conceived through itself, is simply the concept of a thing which is causally independent of everything else; and the concept of mode is of a thing which is causally dependent. (The dependence of properties on a subject is not to be understood as causal dependence.) Now, on our ordinary way of thinking about cause and effect, the cause of a thing is something separate from the thing— the meteor which fell to earth caused the climatic disruption which led to the extinction of the dinosaurs. Spinoza implicitly recognizes this ordinary notion of cause and effect when he distinguishes God's causal relation to his effects as immanent and not transitive (Ip18). One way of understanding Spinoza's notion of immanent causality is that it is the relaton of causality between the essential nature of a subject and its properties. But then to say that one thing is the immanent cause of another presupposes that they are related as subject and property. Thus, if Curley is correct that the relation of substance and mode does not involve that of subject and property, he needs to come up with another way of explaining what Spinoza means when he says that God is the immanent, and not the transitive, cause of everything.

Curley presents his interpretation in terms of what he calls the "model metaphysic," a scheme inspired by the views of the logical atomists.[22] Consider a complete description of the world. Such a description would include first, an indefinite number of singular statements, or statements about individual people and things, e.g., that Socrates lived in ancient Greece; or that this body is heavy. It would also include general statements, statements about classes of things; e.g., that no humans live at the north pole; or that sound travels slower than light. General statements can be divided into two types: nomological generalizations, or those which are strictly universal, and accidental generalizations. The former contain no reference to particular individuals (or times or places) and support counterfactual inference. What we ordinarily think of as scientific laws are the best examples of nomological generalizations. Thus, although the book on my desk is not in motion, I can infer, from the law that a body in motion will continue in motion unless acted on by an outside force, that if it were in motion it would continue to move until it was acted on by some outside force. (This is what is meant by saying that nomological generalizations support counterfactual inference.) Accidental generalizations may contain reference to particular individuals or times or places and do not support counterfactual inference. Thus from "All Jones' assets are in savings accounts" one cannot infer that if Jones were to acquire other assets he would convert them to savings accounts. It is not a law for Jones' assets that they must be in the form of savings accounts as it is a law for bodies that if they are in motion they must continue in motion unless acted on by an outside force. Another difference between accidental and nomological generalizations is that the former can be viewed as equivalent to some conjunction of singular statements and the latter cannot. For example, the statement about Jones' assets is equivalent to the conjunction of "The money Jones has saved from his paycheck for the last ten years is in a savings account," and "The money Jones received from the sale of his condominium is in a savings account," etc. But since nomological generalizations are strictly universal they are of potentially infinite extent, hence, are not equivalent to any conjunction of singular statements.

This complete description of the world mirrors the world. Corresponding to singular statements are singular facts; and corresponding to nomological general statements are "nomological" facts. But there are no special facts corresponding to merely accidental generalizations because these general statements are equivalent to conjunctions of singular statements. (Singular facts are sufficient to account for the truth of accidental generalizations.) The statements comprising the complete description of the world stand in logical relations to one another. Some general statements are logically deducible from others, and singular statements are logically deducible from general ones taken in conjunction with some other singular statement(s). Thus, from the nomological generalization that a body at rest remains at rest unless it acted on by an outside force, we can conclude that very light bodies remain at rest unless they are acted on by an outside force; and taking this statement in conjunction with the statement that Body A is at rest at t and from t to t_1 is not acted on by any outside force, we can conclude that Body A remains at rest from t to t_1.

Assume that the relations among facts which parallel these logical relations among statements are causal relations. On this way of looking at things the world is thoroughly deterministic.[23] Curley suggests applying this model to Spinoza as follows: let the attributes be thought of as the facts corresponding to the highest level nomological generalizations or scientific laws; the infinite modes as those corresponding to the lower level nomological generalizations or derived scientific laws; and finite modes as those corresponding to singular statements. [24]

This interpretation has much to recommend it. For one thing it does justice to those passages where Spinoza talks about causal relations as though they were logical relations, or explicitly compares them to logical relations, as, for example, when he writes that

> infinitely many things in infinitely many modes, i.e., all
> things, have necessarily flowed, or always follow, by the same
> necessity and in the same way as from the natures of a triangle
> it follows, from eternity and to eternity, that its three angles
> are equal to two right angles (Ip17cor2).

It gives us a relatively concrete understanding of the mysterious infinite modes and explains how they are caused by the absolute nature of an attribute. As derivative laws their causation is the factual counterpart of logical consequence. It explains how the two causal chains mentioned above—the rather short chain of infinite causes which begins with the absolute nature of an attribute and proceeds through the infinite modes, and the infinite chain of finite causes—are related, and how the absolute nature of an attribute causally determines finite things. The basic and derivative nomological facts are the factual counterparts of the laws which govern the events in the chain of finite causation. In this way too it assigns a meaning to Spinoza's characterization of God as the immanent cause of things. Immanent causality is indeed a special kind of causality, which corresponds to the relation between a law and the events it governs. God is the immanent cause of everything because the attributes are the factual counterparts of the most basic laws governing everything.

What, if anything, can be said against Curley's interpretation? His claim that for Spinoza the relation between substance and mode is purely a causal relation and not the relation between a subject and its properties implies that Spinoza broke radically from the tradition on this matter. This in itself, however, means little. But with regard to Curley's point that Spinoza's modes are the "wrong logical type" to be predicated of a subject, Spinoza had before him the example of Descartes, who took individual bodies (but not minds) to be modes of substance, not substances, i.e., to be made up of variable qualities of extension.[25] And, as Jonathan Bennett has pointed out, there is a way to construe the claim that one individual is a property (predicated) of another, other than saying that whatever is predicated of the first is predicated of the second. For one individual to be a property of or predicable of another might simply mean that all talk about the first can be reformulated as talk about the second. Thus, Spinoza's claim that there is only one substance or God, and that everything else is a modification of that substance, means, among other things, that all talk of finite individuals can in principle be replaced by talk about God or substance.

According to Bennett, this is in fact just what Spinoza had in mind. Bennett holds that Spinoza followed the tradition on the notion of substance, that the "root idea" of his concept of substance is of "what has properties or is a subject of predication."[26] To this he added the notions of causal and strict logical independence. Substance is what exists in itself and is conceived through itself (Idfn3). From "exists in itself" he concluded that it necessarily exists (Ip7) and is indestructible, hence cannot consist of separable parts. But it also cannot consist of inseparable or conceptual parts, since for it to do so would be contrary to its definition as "conceived through itself." According to Bennett, Spinoza saw that the only extended subject which satisfied the conditions for being substance—having no separable or conceptual parts—was space. The parts of space (regions of space) cannot be "pulled apart;" and the concept of space is not built up by adding together regions of space. Rather the concept of a region of space (a limited space) presupposes that of space. Space, in other words, is one single thing, possessing a unity which can neither be physically decomposed nor decomposed in thought.[27]

On Bennett's view particular bodies are simply the way space is characterized in different regions. A mountain is simply a mountain-shaped region of space characterized by impenetrability, and whatever else is necessary for it to affect other things the way mountains do. The motion of bodies in space is thought of as contiguous regions undergoing change in such a way that a region R at time T closely resembles its contiguous neighbors at T-1 and T+1.   To think of the motion of bodies

> we must associate each object . . . with a spatio-temporally continuous set of place-times, which I call a *string* of them. If there is a string $R_1\text{-}T_1$, $R_2\text{-}T_2$, . . . such that each R_i qualitatively unlike its spatial neighbours at T_i and is qualitatively like the other regions on the string, then that string defines the trajectory of what we call an object in space.[28]
> . . .

Bennett goes on to say that "Spinoza's view is that the movement of things or stuff is, deep down, the passing along of something qualitative—a change in which regions are F and which are not, for suitable values of F."[29] It is like a thaw moving across the countryside. (Another analogy might be the movement of a wave across the ocean. When a wave moves across a body of water, there is no "thing" which is the wave which changes location; rather contiguous areas of the water successively undergo change of shape.)

There is, however, one problem in Bennett's scheme for replacing talk about bodies with talk about space. It is that in order to express in space-talk what we mean when we talk about a particular individual body, we need to be able to identify regions of space. We can say a mountain exists by saying that space is somewhere mountainously characterized; but in order to say that Mt. Everest is 28,000 feet tall, we must be able to refer to or identify a particular mountainous region. In our everyday talk about bodies, we can identify Mt. Everest by its location. But its location is relative to a set of coordinates, which itself is fixed by its relation to something which we can relate to ourselves. Ultimately all reference to individuals involves a reference to here and now, what philosophers call "indexicality." As Bennett himself points out, talk about individual bodies can be replaced by talk about space (a statement about Mt. Everest can only be translated into a statement about space) only if we allow such talk about space to contain indexical terms—ones which allow us to refer to space here and now.[30] Bennett remarks that Spinoza has an hostility to the I-now viewpoint; but worse than that, the notion of "space here, now," contains reference to what is a modification of space, a finite subject. So Bennett has not succeeded in showing how space talk could replace talk about bodies, and has not shown how individual bodies can be viewed as properties of the one extended substance, space.

Both Curley's and Bennett's interpretations work well, if not perfectly, as accounts of how Spinoza conceived the relation between substance considered under one of its attributes and modes. I shall not attempt to adjudicate between them, but I shall briefly consider the appeal and limitations of each. For Curley the unity of the diverse modes of substance considered under a single attribute consists entirely in the fact that modes are governed by a single system of laws. Extended substance is identified with its attribute, extension, and the attribute is construed as the set of facts corresponding to the set of highest level laws governing finite bodies. Substance as a subject or substratum has dropped out—it is not needed to explain how things are all in the same substance, or how God is an immanent cause. Curley's Spinoza is thus radically modern, anticipating empiricist critiques of the notion of substance, excising unnecessary notions from his metaphysical system. Bennett's interpretation of space as substance portrays a less radical Spinoza, one who accepts the traditional notion of substance as a subject and substratum in which modes exist, for whom the unity of diverse modes of a single attribute is not merely their subjection to a single system of laws, but is also their being in a single subject. Bennett's interpretation is more consistent than Curley's with Spinoza's characterization of modes as "the affections of substance" (Idfn5).[31] And while it is true (as Curley argues) that the assumption of Bennett's interpretation—that ultimately talk of modes could be replaced by talk of substance—is wrong, it also seems true, as Bennett maintains, that Spinoza wouldn't have seen that.[32].

Summary

Unlike earlier substance theorists, Spinoza reasoned that there is only one substance, God, and that everything else—rocks, trees, individual human bodies and minds—is a modification of that substance. He reached this conclusion via an argument based partly on the definition of God as substance "consisting of an infinity of attributes." An attribute is a conceptually basic, essential property of subtance, which is general in the sense that every modification of substance must be conceived in terms of some attribute. Rocks and human bodies must be conceived in terms of extension; minds must be conceived in terms of thought. How the one substance can consist of an infinity of independent attributes, or how reality can consist of fundamentally diverse kinds of thing and still be one, is a serious problem for Spinoza's monistic metaphysics.

The relation of substance to mode in Spinoza has traditionally been taken to be that of a subject to its prperties. E. M. Curley rejects this, holding instead that it should be understood along the lines of the relation of the most basic laws of physics to the movements of individual bodies, which on Curley's view is a purely causal relation. Jonathan Bennett, on the other hand, accepts the traditional view, but maintains that for Spinoza extended substance is space, and that the modifications of substance are simply differently qualified regions of space.

Endnotes

---

[1] References to Spinoza's *Ethics* will be given in the text, using the following system of abbreviations: upper case Roman numerals (I – V) stand for one of the five Parts of the *Ethics*; "p"

stands for "proposition;" "dfn" for "definition;" "ax" for "axiom" "dem" for "demonstration;" "cor" for "corollary;" "post" for "postulate," and "sch" for "scholium." Thus, "IIp13cor,sch" indicates the scholium to the corollary to proposition 13 of part II. All quotations are from Edwin Curley, *The Collected Works of Spinoza*, I.

[2] 2a11-13.

[3] 2b5-17; see also 2b35.

[4] 4a10-12.

[5] "Author's Replies to the Second Set of Objections" in Cottingham, Stoothoff and Murdoch, v. II, 114. Future references to this English translation of Descartes' writings will be indicated by "CSM."

[6] *Principles* I, 51, in CSM, I, 210.

[7] *Principles* I, 52, in CSM, I, 210.

[8] "Synopsis" of the *Meditations*, in CSM II, 10.

[9] In the *Principles of Philosophy* I, 56, Descartes characterizes the term "mode" as meaning a variable property or quality of substance (CSM I, 211-12.).

[10] I have presented the steps of the argument in a different order than that of their occurrence in Spinoza's demonstration.

[11] *Principles of Philosophy* I, 53; CSM I, 210-11.

[12] My discussion of this question is indebted to Charlton, 514-15, and Delahunty, 112-14.

[13] Curley 1986 provides a good discussion of what is at stake as well as the evidence on both sides of this issue. How we can know the definitions are true is discussed below, in chapter 6, pp. 87 – 88.

[14] This is the reasoning expressed in Descartes' argument for the real distinction between mind and body in *Meditation* VI (CSM II, 54), and in the *Principles of Philosophy* I, 60 (CSM I, 213).

[15] CSM II, 28-31.

[16] *Proslogion*, chapter 2.

[17] Some commentators, however, have interpreted Spinoza as explaining the appearance of diversity as illusion. H. A. Wolfson, for example, took him to hold that the apparent multiplicity of the attributes of substance was a figment of human subjectivity (Wolfson, I, 148-56). H. H. Joachim seems inclined to view him as holding that our apprehension of distinct modes of substance is illusory (Joachim, 107-122).

[18] "Author's Replies to the Second Set of Objections," CSM II, 114; *Principles of Philosophy* I, 53, 56, CSM I, 210-12.

[19] Curley 1969, 18, 37-38; 1988, 31.

[20] Curley 1969, 18; 1988, 31- 36.

[21] Curley 1969, 36-43; 1988, 31.

[22] Curley 1969, 50-55.

[23] Curley assumes that all the singular statements are entailed by general nomological ones, taken in conjunction with other singular statements.

[24] Curley 1969, 55 – 74; 1988, 42 – 48.

[25] "Synopsis" of the *Meditations*, CSM II, 10. Some commentators discount Descartes' denial of substantiality to the body in this passage, because he commonly refers to the body as a substance. But I take the passage to mean that strictly the body is not a substance; and I take it seriously because it seems to me to be an implication of his doctrine concerning substance.

[26] Bennett 1984, 55.

[27] Bennett 1984, 81-88.

[28] Bennett 1984, 89.

[29] Bennett 1984, 89-90.

[30] Bennett 1984, 95-96.

[31] In the definition of mode, "affections" is a translation of *affectiones*, which might also be rendered as "states."

[32] Curley argues at length against Bennett's interpretation in his "On Bennett's Interpretation of Spinoza's Monism." Bennett counters in his "Spinoza's Monism: A Reply to Curley." Both appear in Yovel, 1991.

3

Mind and Body

The Union of Mind and Body

According to Descartes the mind (a thinking substance) and body (a "certain configuration of limbs and other accidents") are two really distinct entities, capable of existing apart from another. Thus, "the decay of the body does not imply the destruction of the mind." [1] The essential functions of the mind—thinking and willing—are independent of the body, and similarly, those of a living body—that it be capable of various sorts of complex movement—can be accounted for by the same mechanical principles that govern non-living ones. Non-human animals, which lack a mind or soul, are merely highly complex machines. The principle of all movement of a living body is a kind of heat or fire in the heart, which causes the circulation of the blood and "animal spirits," a volatile fluid substance.[2] Descartes describes a complex network of nerves "which are like little threads or tubes coming from the brain and containing, like the brain itself, a very fine air or wind which is called the 'animal spirits'."[3] This neural structure explains how the brain is able to communicate with the rest of the body, and provides the basis for explaining all animal and much human behavior on a purely physiological, stimulus-response model. For example, motions produced in the eye by an external stimulus are transmitted via the nerves to the brain, where they in turn cause "the spirits to make their way to certain muscles rather than others, . . . so causing them to move our limbs."[4]

Despite their essential independence of one another, in this life mind and body are intimately connected:

> Nature also teaches me, by these sensations of pain, hunger, thirst and so on, that I am not merely present in my body as a sailor is present in a ship, but that I am very closely joined and, as it were, intermingled with it, so that I and the body form a unit. If this were not so, I, who am nothing but a thinking thing, would not feel pain when the body was hurt, but would perceive the damage purely by the intellect, just as a sailor perceives by sight if anything in his ship is broken. . . . [T]hese sensations . . . are nothing but confused modes of thinking which arise from the union and, as it were, intermingling of the mind with the body.[5]

In *The Passions of the Soul*, I, Descartes attempted to explain the union of mind and body, or to show how the body is able to act on the mind, causing sensations and passions (states of consciousness) in the mind; and how the mind is able to move the body (voluntary movement). He maintained that while "the soul is joined to the whole body" it "directly exercises its functions" in the "innermost part of the brain, which is a certain very small gland situated in the middle of the brain's substance. . . ."[6] He described this mechanism in *The Passions* I, 34:

> [T]he small gland which is the principal seat of the soul is suspended within the cavities containing these spirits, so that it can be moved by them in as many different ways as there are perceptible differences in the objects [of perception]. But it can also be moved in various different ways by the soul, whose nature is such that it receives as many different impressions—that is, it has as many diffferent perceptions as there occur different movements in this gland. And conversely, the mechanism of our body is so constructed that simply by this gland's being moved in any way by the soul or by any other cause, it drives the surrounding spirits towards the pores of the brain, which direct them through the nerves to the muscles; and in this way the gland makes the spirits move the limbs.[7]

For Spinoza, the notion that the mind—something immaterial and unextended—should move or be moved by a body was unintelligible:

> What, I ask does he [Descartes] understand by the union of Mind and Body? What clear and distinct conception does he have of a thought so closely united to some little portion of quantity? Indeed, I wish he had explained this union by its

proximate cause. But he had conceived the Mind to be so distinct from the Body that he could not assign any singular cause, either of this union or of the Mind itself. Instead, it was necessary for him to have recourse to the cause of the whole Universe, i.e., to God.

> Again, I should like very mch to know how many degrees of motion the Mind can give to that pineal gland, and how great a force is required to hold it in suspense (V, Preface).

By Spinoza's lights, Descartes simply failed to explain the union of mind and body. His own account of their union is set in terms of a more general account of the relation between modes of the attribute thought, and those of extension and whatever other attributes there may be. The main features of the general account are as follows.

First, it asserts a kind of equality between thought and the other attributes. Just as all possible things are produced by God or follow from each of his attributes (Ip16), so God has ideas of all such things (IIp3). Second, it denies the possibility of causal interaction between modes of different attributes. Since an idea is simply a mode of thought, it must be understood through thought alone, apart from any other attribute. Thus, by Iax4, that "the knowledge of an effect depends on, and involves, the knowledge of the cause," it follows that an idea cannot be caused by anything other than an idea or modification of thought (IIp5). The same reasoning applies equally to the modes of other attributes: "The modes of each attribute have God for their cause only in so far as he is considered under the attribute of which they are modes, and not insofar as he is considered under any other attribute" (IIp6). Finally, the account asserts that "The order and connection of ideas is the same as the order and connection of things" (IIp7). Since the demonstration of this proposition merely cites Iax4, that "the knowledge of an effect depends on, and involves, knowledge of the cause," he evidently means that the causal order of ideas parallels the causal order of things, that the cause of an idea of x is the idea of the cause of x. As we shall see the general principles expressed by IIp6 and IIp7--that there is no causal interaction between modes of different attributes, but that the order of ideas parallels that of things—play tremendously important roles in Spinoza's general metaphysical doctrine and in his thinking about the mind and knowledge.

Whereas Descartes held human beings to be thinking substances causally linked with bodies, Spinoza (as we should expect, given his substance monism) maintained that "The being of substance does not pertain to the essence of man" (IIp10), but rather that "the essence of man is constituted by certain modifications of God's attributes"

(IIp10cor). A particular human mind is simply the idea—God's idea—of a particular human body (IIp11, 13). As such it is "part of the infinite intellect of God" (IIp11cor).

It may seem odd for Spinoza to say that the mind *is* an idea; ordinarily we think of the mind as the subject which has ideas, not as being one. The Cartesian notion of the mind as the finite thinking substance in which ideas exist as modes or states thus appears to be more consistent with our ordinary way of thinking and talking about the mind. But Spinoza's conception of the mind as an idea is a consequence of (a) his substance monism, according to which everything other than God must be a modification of some attribute of God; and (b) his taking ideas as the basic kind of modification in the attribute of thought, thus putting them on a par with bodies in extension. That ideas are the basic type of modification of thought is asserted by IIax3, that

> There are no modes of thinking, such as love, desire, or
> whatever is designated by the word affects of th mind, unless
> there is in the same Individual the idea of the thing loved,
> desired, etc. But there can be an idea, even though there is no
> other mode of thinking.

Thus, in Spinoza's system there is nothing for the human mind to be except an idea. The first part of the demonstration of IIp11 expresses this line of thought:

> The essence of man (by P10C) is constituted by certain
> modifications of God's attributes, viz. (by A2) by modes of
> thinking, of all of which (by A3) the idea is prior in nature,
> and when it is given, the other modes (to which the idea is
> prior in nature) must be in the same individual (by A3). And
> therefore an idea is the first thing that constitutes the being of
> a human Mind.

Our discomfort with reconceptualizing the mind along the lines of Spinoza's account stems at least partly from the fact that it seems to threaten what we think of as our individuality. If "I" am an idea in the mind of God, then "I" am merely a state of another subject, and there is no "I" (or I am not myself an individual subject). One way to deal with this problem is to adopt Curley's interpretation of the relation between substance and mode. On that interpretation finite modes are causally dependent on substance, but they are not related to substance as states of a subject. Rather, as individuals, they are subjects. Keeping Curley's interpretation in mind, it may seem odd that Spinoza should call the basic modifications of the attribute of thought ideas, since in the Cartesian tradition, as well as in our usage, ideas are thought to require a subject in which they reside. But if ideas are not thought of as

34

themselves residing in a subject, that removes one impediment to thinking of the mind as an idea.

Even accepting the more traditional interpretation of the relation of substance and mode as subject and state or property, however, it does not follow that because the mind is an idea in the mind of God it cannot itself be an individual subject. For Spinoza what makes the mind an individual subject is that it is the idea of the body, which is an individual subject. In order to understand this, we need to look more closely at the relation between ideas and their objects, and at the nature of the object of the mind—the body..

Ideas are what may be called primary representors. To understand what this means, consider how words, which are simply sounds or marks on paper, can represent things. A particular sound or set of marks does not naturally represent anything, but only by convention, i.e., only insofar as the speakers of a language invest it with a meaning. By contrast, ideas for Spinoza are, by nature or essentially, representative of or "about" something, or have content. An idea cannot lack this representational quality, and its very nature—what it is—depends on its content or object. In seventeenth century terms, ideas have "objective reality," in modern terms, "intentionality."

As an idea, then, the mind bears an essential, but noncausal, relation to its object, the body. The essential linkage between the mind and body in Spinoza has three important aspects. In the first place the existence of the mind necessarily parallels that of the body. Thus, Spinoza continues the demonstration of IIp11 (above) inferring further that the idea which constitutes the mind is

> not the idea of a thing which does not exist. For then (by P8C) the idea itseif could not be said to exist. Therefore it will be the idea of a thing which actually exists. Bu not of an infinite thing. For an infinite thing (by IP21 and 2) must always exist necessarily. . . . . Therefore, the first thing that constitutes the actual being of a human Mind is the idea of a singular thing which actually exists.

The second aspect of the essential linkage between mind and body is that as an idea the mind is necessarily individuated by its object. As a mode of extension the body is not a *substantial* individual, but it is nonetheless an individual insofar as it has a distinct and specifiable nature which is more or less enduring over time. Spinoza discusses the individuation of bodies in the material he presents "concerning the nature of bodies" following IIp13sch. Although the simplest bodies are distinguished from one another "only by motion and rest, speed and slowness," what distinguishes a complex body (such as the human body) from other things is either that its component parts "are so onstrained by other bodies that they lie upon one another," or if they move, that "they communicate their motions to eachother in a certain fixed manner" (IIax2, and dfn, following lemma 3). Complex individuals such as the human body are thus able to undergo many types of change, including replacement of their component parts (as in nutrition and respiration, growth and diminution, and change of place) while remaining the same identical thing (lemmas 4 - 7). Insofar as the body can remain the same individual while undergoing change, it is properly thought of as a subject of properties, i.e., a subject in which different qualities come to be or cease to exist (e.g., size, shape).

As the idea of something with a distinct and specifiable nature—a complex individual—the mind is similarly a complex individual (IIp15). And as the idea of a thing which is able to endure through many types of change, the mind also is a subject of properties, i.e., is a subject in which different ideas come to be or cease to exist. Like the body it is not a substantial individual, not the ultimate subject of change or different states. But it is an individual subject, nonetheless.

The third aspect of the essential linkage between mind and body in Spinoza is that mental processes and the abilities and limitations of the mind can be explained in terms of bodily processes and abilities and limitations. All things are "animate" or God has an idea of each thing just as he has the idea of the human body; but

> Ideas differ among themselves as the objects themselves do, . . . one is more excellent than the other, and contains more reality, just as the object of the one is more excellent than the object of the other and contains more reality. And so to determine what is the difference between the human Mind and the others, and how it surpasses them, it is necessary for us. . . to know the nature of its object, i.e., the human Body. . . .
> [I]n proportion as a Body is more capable than others of doing many things at once, or being acted on in many ways at once, so its Mind is more capable than others of perceiving many things at once. And in proportion as the actions of a body depend more on itself alone, and as other bodies concur with it less in acting, so its mind is more capable of understanding distinctly (IIp13cor, sch).

I turn now to Spinoza's treatment of cognitive mental processes and the extent of human knowledge.

Cognition

Sense Perception and Imagination

Descartes explains our ability to perceive external objects as follows: an external object causes motion in some external organ of sense, which in turn causes a motion in the nerves, which in its turn causes the pineal gland to move in a certain way, which causes a certain sensation in the mind. Since Spinoza denies that there can be causal relations between modes of different attributes, he must offer a different explanation. His account relies on two basic doctrines: the parallelism thesis, that "the order and connection of ideas is the same as the order and connection of things," and the conception of the mind as God's idea of the body. By parallelism, God has the idea of what happens in any object only insofar as he has the idea of that object (IIp9cor). It follows from this that the ideas of what happens in the body must be in the human mind, or, as Spinoza paraphrases in IIp12, the human mind perceives whatever happens in the human body. When external bodies act on our organs of sense, the state or modification of the sense organ (and nervous system) that they produce is a result of both the nature of the external body and our own body. Spinoza reasons, therefore, that the idea of that state represents ("involves") both the nature of the human body and that of the external body, although in a confused way (IIp16). Thus, because the mind directly perceives what happens in the body, it indirectly perceives external bodies (IIp16cor1).

The ability to imagine things which are not present and memory are similarly explained in terms of the mind's having ideas of the states of the body. As long as the body is affected in a way that "involves the nature of an external body," the mind will regard that body as "actually existing or as present to it" (IIp17). Thus, we can imagine things which are not present or do not actually exist so long as our body is in the state it would be in if the thing we imagine were actually present (IIp17and cor). The association of ideas involved in memory is simply "a certain connection of ideas involving the nature of thing which are outside the human Body—a connection that is in the mind according to the order and connection of the affections of the human Body" (IIp18sch). Spinoza explains that he uses the term "image" to refer to the affections (states) of the human body "whose ideas present external bodies as present to us;" and his general term for thinking which involves such ideas is "imagination" (IIp17cor,sch). Thus sense perception, memory, and dreaming, as well as imagining things which do not exist or are not present are all imaginative functions of the mind.

Spinoza distinguishes between the idea of Peter

> which constitutes the essence of Peter's mind, and the idea of Peter which is in another man, say in Paul. For the former directly explains the essence of Peter's body, and does not involve existence except as long as Peter exists; but the latter indicates the constitution of Paul's body more than Peter's nature, therefore while that constitution of Paul's body lasts, Paul's mind will regard Peter as present to itself, even though Peter does not exist (IIp17sch).

He might have drawn the same contrast between the idea of Peter which "constitutes the essence of Peter's mind" and "directly explains the essence of Peter's body" and Peter's own idea of his body. The idea of the body which constitutes a person's mind—e.g., God's idea of Peter's body—is not identical with any idea by which the person represents his body to himself or perceives his body. As is the case with external bodies, we perceive our own bodies only indirectly, through the ideas of the states of the body which are present in the mind, whose objects are directly perceived by us (IIp19 and dem).

What the mind can perceive or in any way represent to itself is limited to what can be represented by ideas which are in God's idea of the human body. And so far the only ideas which have been shown to be in God's idea of the human body—the human mind—are the ideas of the body's modifications. In order to explain how the mind is able to perceive its own ideas and itself (introspection) Spinoza draws on a deeper aspect of the relation of mind and body. Since God has the ideas of all things which can be conceived through each of his attributes, and since ideas are modes of the attribute thought, God must have the idea of every idea, including the idea of the mind. By the parallelism doctrine, the idea of the mind must be "related to God in the same way as the idea or knowledge of the human body" (IIp20). And just as the mind is united to the body through the body's being the object of the mind, the idea of the mind is united to the mind through the mind's being its object (IIp21).

We have referred to IIp7 as asserting that the causal order of ideas parallels that of the modes of extension (or of other attributes). In the scholium to IIp7cor Spinoza appears to express a significantly stronger doctrine, that ideas are identical with their objects, from which the parallelism of the causal orders in different attributes follows as a consequence. In IIp21sch he refers back to this passage as a basis for asserting that

[T]he idea of the Body, and the Body, i.e.(by P13), the Mind and the Body, are one and the same Individual, which is conceived now under the attribute of Thought, and now under the attribute of Extension. So the idea of the Mind and the Mind itself are one and the same thing, which is conceived under one and the same attribute, viz., Thought.

Since, by parallelism, "the ideas of the ideas of the affections follow in God in the same way and are related to God in the same way as the ideas themselves of the affections" (IIp22dem), it follows that these ideas of ideas will be in God's idea of the human mind, and therefore (by the identity of this idea with the mind), in the mind itself. Thus the mind perceives its ideas (IIp22), and itself, through its ideas (IIp23).

Sense Perception (and Introspection) as Inadequate Knowledge

Spinoza assesses the knowledge we have of our mind and body and external bodies which we have through the ideas of our own body's modifications (and through the ideas of these ideas) as inadequate, or mutilated and confused. It is confused in that the ideas of the modifications of the body do not involve a clear differentiation among the properties belonging to the external object, those belonging to our own body, and those belonging to the state which results from the external body's acting on our body (IIp16cor2). And it is mutilated, in that the ideas of the bodily modifications only partially represent both the body and external objects. For example, the idea of the human body which we derive from our idea of some bodily modification is only of the body as affected in a certain way, and not of it as capable of being affected in many different ways (IIp27 and dem).

In IIdfn4 Spinoza defines an adequate idea as one which "considered in itself, without relation to an object, has all the properties or intrinsic denominations of a true idea." He goes on to add in explanation that by "intrinsic" he means to exclude what is "extrinsic," the agreement of a true idea with its object. What these "intrinsic denominations" are is not spelled out in the *Ethics*, but in correspondence he indicated that by an adequate idea he meant one from which all the properties of the thing could be inferred, and which, as a necessary condition for this, involved the cause of the thing.[8] The reasoning behind the second requirement is that since a thing derives all its properties from its cause, the idea of a thing from which all its properties can be inferred must involve the cause of the thing. Following out this line of thought, since the complete cause of the thing is required to produce the thing with all its properties, the idea from which all the properties can be inferred must involve the complete cause of the thing. Further, if the cause of the thing depends on some further cause (i.e., if it is not self-caused), then this too must be involved in the adequate idea of the thing, or the idea will not involve the complete cause. What this comes to is that an adequate idea is one which involves the complete and ultimate cause of the thing. To have adequate knowledge of a thing is to understand fully what a thing is and why it is what it is.

Because God's mind (the counterpart in thought of the infinite individual which is nature) contains the ideas of all things, and the causal order of ideas replicates that of things, each thing is perfectly—adequately and truly—represented in God's mind (IIp32). Our minds, however, are merely finite parts of God's mind. Hence Spinoza writes

> [W]hen we say that the human Mind perceives this or that, we are saying nothing but that God, not insofar as he is infinite, but insofar as he is explained through the nature of the human Mind, or insofar as he constitutes the essence of the human Mind, has this or that idea; and when we say that God has this or that idea, not only insofar as he constitutes the nature of the human Mind, but insofar as he also has the idea of another thing together with the human Mind, then we say that the human Mind perceives the thing only partially, or inadequately (IIp11cor).

The human mind does not have adequate knowledge of its body or its parts, external bodies, the body's modification, itself, or its ideas because the ideas of the causes of all these things are beyond the scope of the mind (IIp24, 25, 26, 27, 28,29). They are in God insofar as he constitutes the minds of other things. Indeed, insofar as all of these things are finite modes which ultimately depend on an endless chain of prior causes, adequate knowledge of them will be in God only insofar as he has the ideas of all these prior causes (see IIp30dem).

Adequate Knowledge: Reason and the Common Notions

The mind does, however, have certain adequate knowledge. "Those things which are common to all, and which are equally in the part and in the whole, can only be conceived adequately" (IIp38). This is because the ideas of such things are necessarily adequate in God in so far as he has any idea—including those of the affections of the body—and therefore insofar as he constitutes the mind of anything—including the human mind (IIp38dem). Why this is so is made clear by the reference in IIp38cor to lemma 2, which indicates that what Spinoza has in mind by "things which are common to all" are things like extension and (degree of) motion and rest. As an attribute extension must be involved in the idea of any of its modes, and it has no further cause, but is the cause both of itself and its (immediate) infinite mode, motion and rest. These are things, therefore, of which the mind cannot fail to have an adequate idea, since their cause is adequately represented in the mind. Since they are adequate these ideas must be true, because for an idea to be adequate in our mind is for God to have that idea insofar as he constitutes our mind; and in God all ideas are true (IIp32, 33 and dem).

Because what is common to all does not constitute the essence of any singular (finite) thing (IIp37), the common notions provide only general or universal knowledge things. But Spinoza goes to some length in IIp40sch1 to distinguish the common notions from our ideas of what is designated by transcendental terms such as "being" and "thing" and universals such as man, horse, dog. Both transcendental and universal notions have their origin in imaginative thinking and result from the body's being incapable of forming more than a certain number of distinct images at one time. When that number is exceeded, the images will be confused with one another. Since the mind is able to imagine distinctly at the same time only as many bodies as there can be images in the body,

> when the images in the body are completely confused, the Mind also will imagine all bodies confusedly, without any distinction, and comprehend them as if under one attribute, viz., under the attribute of Being, Thing, etc. . . . these terms signify ideas that are confused in the highest degree.

Universal notions arise from the same cause, but represent a lesser degree of confusion. The power of the body to form distinct images is not entirely overcome, but only

> to the point where the Mind can imagine neither slight differences of the singular [men] (such as the color and size of each one, etc.) nor their determinate number, and imagines distinctly only what they all agree in, insofar as they affect the body.

Such universal notions vary subjectively from one individual to another, depending on what the person's body has been affected by, and the what her mind more easily imagines or remembers (also a function of the body). Thus those who have more often regarded men's stature with wonder will understand by the word *man* an animal of erect stature. But those who have been accustomed to consider something else, will form another common image of men— e.g., that man is an animal capable of laughter, or a featherless biped, or a rational animal.

Like our imaginative knowledge of singular things, universal notions formed in the above way, i.e., "from singular things which have been represented to us through the senses in a way that is mutilated, confused, and without order for the intellect" are only inadequate representations of things (Iip40sch2). And because Spinoza views our understanding of language as simply a matter of the mind's associating ideas in a way which parallels a linkage in the states of the body (e.g., the state of the body which results from hearing the word "apple" is linked to its being affected with the image of an apple), he also thinks that knowledge we have simply "from signs" or from reading or hearing about something, is inadequate. Spinoza groups these two kinds of inadequate knowledge together in IIp40sch2, calling them "knowledge of the first kind, opinion, or imagination."

In contrast to all imaginative representations, the common notions do not vary with the nature and circumstances of the individual knower, but rather as adequate ideas, accurately represent their objects (what is common to all, and equally in the part and in the whole). They are the basis for what Spinoza calls reason or knowledge of the second kind (IIp40sch.2). The second kind of knowledge includes physics, the science of extended things or bodies, and psychology, the science of thinking things or minds. In addition to these two kinds of knowledge Spinoza mentions a third, which he calls "intuition" and which he describes as proceeding from "an adequate knowledge of the essence of certain attributes of God to an adequate knowledge of the essence of things." The basis of intuition is the same as that of reason—knowledge of an attribute. But, in contrast to reason, which is a kind of general knowledge of things, Spinoza's characterization of intuition implies that it is a kind of knowledge of individuals.

Because knowledge of the first kind includes all that involves or is based on inadequate ideas, it is the "only cause of falsity," while "knowledge of the second and of the third kind is necessarily true" (IIp41and dem). It may seem odd for Spinoza to speak of knowledge as the cause of falsity, but two points can be made which cast light on this. First, Spinoza regards falsity not as something positive (IIp33), but merely as "the privation of knowledge which inadequate, or mutilated and confused, ideas, involve" (IIp35). "All ideas insofar as they are related to God, are true" (IiI32); and falsity, like inadequacy and confusion is relative to a particular mind, arising from that mind's lack of knowledge (IIp36dem).

Second, because all ideas insofar as they are related to God are true, every idea no matter how inadequately it may represent a thing in some particular mind, even in that mind gives some indication of reality. Thus, no idea is absolutely false.

Spinoza's views on sense perception and reason appear partly to coincide with, and partly to diverge from, those of Descartes. Like Descartes, Spinoza holds that sense perception does not provide us with insight into the fundamental natures of things. For such understanding, we need the common notions of reason, which on the surface at least, seem rather similar to Cartesian innate ideas. There are, however, important differences between Spinoza's common notions and Descartes' innate ideas. In the first place, Spinoza's common notions are in the mind *naturally*, or in it in virtue of its very nature. The mind, for Spinoza, is the idea of an actually existing body. As such it necessarily has the ideas of or perceives whatever happens in that body; and insofar as it has any idea of a bodily modification, it must have an adequate representation of what is common to all bodies. Cartesian minds, by contrast, do not by nature have the ideas of extension, size, shape, motion, etc., which are the basis for Cartesian science, but God has to put them into the mind by a special act. (For Descartes, it is the knowledge that God puts these ideas in our mind that assures us that they are true.) The same contrast holds between the two philosophers with respect to the idea of God. According to Descartes God implants in every soul the idea of himself as the "mark of the craftsman stamped on his work."[9] But for Spinoza the adequate knowledge of an attribute which every idea of an actually existing finite thing involves, also—by definition of an attribute—constitutes knowledge of the essence of God. Thus, that "the human mind has an adequate knowledge of God's eternal and infinite essence" also has a natural explanation (IIp47; see also IIp45 and 46).

It is important to note also with respect to Spinoza's common notions that they are not merely in the mind by virtue of its nature as the idea of an actually existing body, but that they are dependent on sense experience, i.e., on there being in the mind an idea of some modification of its body. Some commentators seem to me to have made too much of this dependence on experience. For example, Genevieve Lloyd writes that for Spinoza

> The mind, as idea of a human body, has a past . . . .Its having a
> past is due to the human capacity to compare different bodily
> traces. That capacity makes possible the formation of
> common notions and hence the passage from imagination to

reason. Imagination makes reason possible by enabling the mind to have a past in a way that goes beyond mere existence through time. The mind, as idea of a body which endures, retains its past: and this retention allows it to make the comparisons between experiences which will issue in common notions. . . . [T]his crucial capacity for abstraction is not independent of body.[10]

But I am not aware of any place in Spinoza's writings where he states or implies that the mind must compare ideas of bodily "traces" in order to determine what is common to all. On the contrary, he appears to reason in IIp38dem that since what is "common to all" and "equally in the part and in the whole" is involved in the idea of any modification of extension, any idea alone can yield its concept. That Spinoza held the source of knowledge to lie in sense experience in the way we have described shows that his doctrine is not typically rationalist; but it is also not so radically empiricist as Lloyd's interpretation implies.

Judgment, Error and the Will

Descartes' theory of judgment is presented in *Meditation* IV where its purpose is to forestall a potentially fatal objection to his proof that God exists and is no deceiver. The objection would run as follows: if I am the creation of a perfect or non-deceitful God, the I ought to be incapable of error or false judgment. But I know from experience that I am prone to error; therefore, I am not the creation of a perfect (non-deceitful) God. The objection is the intellectual version of what is commonly known "problem of evil," which is to explain how a perfectly good and omnipotent God can allow evil (error) to exist. Part of Descartes solution to the problem is to present an analysis of judgment and error which makes us, not God, responsible for our errors.

According to Descartes, making a judgment involves the two separate mental faculties of intellect and will. By means of the intellect we perceive the ideas which are subjects for possible judgments; by means of the will we affirm or deny what is contained in an idea. Judgment consists in affirming or denying what the intellect perceives. Since the will is free, judgments are also free, although Descartes' characterization of what can count as "free" affirmations and judgments seems somewhat counterintuitive. He holds that if our will is compelled either by God or by a clear and distinct perception to affirm something, such an affirmation or judgment counts as free. In cases where we do not clearly and distinctly perceive a thing, however,

Descartes holds that our will is not compelled, thus that we are "free" in a less contentious sense to affirm or deny the thing or to suspend judgment altogether (although according to Descartes, this is the lowest grade of freedom). Ideas in themselves are neither true nor false; rather the vehicle of truth and falsity is judgment.[11] Error or false judgment, according to Descartes, occurs when we freely choose to affirm or deny a thing which we do not perceive clearly and distinctly. Since we always have the option in cases where we lack a clear and distinct perception of a thing to suspend judgment, error or false judgment is due to us, not God.

Since Spinoza's conception of God's perfection excludes both his possession of a free will and any kind of moral qualities, Spinoza does not have the same need as Descartes to show that error is not due to God. Nonetheless there are reasons why he needs to explain the occurrence of error. In the first place our tendency to err or make false judgments is a significant fact of human existence. Second, we have a practical need to understand how erroneous judgments differ from true ones so we can avoid the former; and third, we need to understand the difference between erroneous judgments and true ones so we do not fall prey to the type of skeptical argument which rests on our inability to distinguish a true judgment from a false one.

Unlike Descartes, Spinoza takes truth to be a property of ideas (Iax6; IIp32, 33, 34, 35, 43). Further, he holds that "All ideas are true in so far as they are related to God" (IIp32), because by his parallelism doctrine all of God's ideas agree with their objects (IIp7, Iax6). From this it follows that all of our adequate ideas are true (IIp34), since for us to have an adequate idea of a thing is simply for God to have the idea of that thing insofar as he constitutes our mind. Falsity, therefore, is nothing positive in ideas (IIp33), but rather, "Falsity consists in the privation of knowledge which inadequate ideas, that is, fragmentary and confused ideas, involve" (IIp35). What Spinoza means by this is illustrated in the scholium following the proposition, where he gives two examples:

> men are deceived in that they think themselves free. . . an opinion which consists only in this, that they are conscious of their actions and ignorant of the causes by which they are determined. This, then, is their idea of freedom—that they do not know any cause of their actions. . . . .

> Similarly, when we look at the sun, we imagine it as about 200 feet away from us, an error that does not consist simply in this imagining, but in the fact that while we imagine it in this way, we are ignorant of its true distance and of the cause of this imagining. For even if we later come to know

that it is more than 600 diameters of the earth away from us,
we nevertheless imagine it as near. For we imagine the sun so
near not because we do not know its true distance, but because
an affection of our body involves the essence of the sun
insofar as our body is affected by the sun.

Spinoza seems to be saying here that considered in itself no idea is
false, but false belief or error consists in having inadequate—
fragmentary and confused—ideas, which are not recognized as such, or
having such ideas outside of a context in which they are overridden by
others. A similar analysis of error is found in IIp17sch, where talking
about the mind's imagining things which in fact are not present he
writes:

[T]he imaginations of the Mind, considered in themselves
contain no error, *or* . . . the Mind does not err from the fact
that it imagines, but only insofar as it is considered to lack an
idea that excludes the existence of those things that it imagines
to be present to it.

Descartes' analysis of error presupposes three theses which
Spinoza explicitly denies in IIp48 and 49 and their scholia. The first is
his doctrine that the will is free. Spinoza expresses his rejection of this
doctrine in IIp48, where he writes that "In the Mind there is no
absolute, or free, will, but the Mind is determined to will this or that by
a cause which is also determined by another, and this again by another,
and so to infinity." This proposition is a consequence of his general
metaphysical doctrine that every finite mode is determined to existence
and action by another, which is in turn determined by another, and so
on ad infinitum (Ip28).

More radically, Spinoza also denies that acts of will (volitions) are
distinct from perceptions (ideas). He expresses this in IIp49, which
states that "In the Mind there is no volition, or affirmation and
negation, except that which the idea involves insofar as it is an idea,"
adding in the corollary that the will and the intellect—singular volitions
and ideas—are "one and the same." Spinoza argues for the identity of
will and intellect by attempting to establish (i) that an affirmation must
involve an idea; and (ii) an idea must involve an affirmation. The first
point seems plausible and unproblematic. One must have an idea say,
of a triangle, in order to affirm anything about a triangle or that a
triangle exists. But the second is not so obvious. Why can't one just
have an idea of a thing without either affirming (or denying) anything
about it or that it exists? Spinoza's official argument, given in the
demonstration to IIp49, fails for a number of reasons. But he has
another line of thought which does offer support for his claim that
every idea involves an affirmation. It appears in his response to an

anticipated objection to the view, that "experience seems to teach nothing more clearly than that we can suspend our judgment so as not to assent to things we perceive." Spinoza answers the objection first by giving his own analysis of so-called "suspension of judgment":

> [W]hen we say that someone suspends judgment, we are saying nothing but that he sees that he does not perceive the thing adequately. Suspension of judgment, therefore, is really a perception, not [an act of] free will (IIp49cor,sch).

He continues

> To understand this clearly, let us conceive a child imagining a winged horse, and not perceiving anything else. Since this imagination involves the existence of the horse (by P17C), and the child does not perceive anything else that excludes the existence of the horse, he will necessarily regard the horse as present. Nor will he be able to doubt its existence, though he will not be certain of it (IIp49cor,sch).

Spinoza's reference here to IIp17cor seems to show that what he has in mind is that for someone to imagine a winged horse a*nd nothing else which excludes the existence of the horse*, is for his body to be affected in the way it would be affected by an actual winged horse. Thus, to imagine a winged horse *and nothing else which excludes the existence of the horse* is also to be in the same state of mind as one would be in if one perceived an actual winged horse. And since the latter involves an affirmation or assent, so must the former.[12]

Given that Spinoza rejects the Cartesian doctrine that volitons or acts of will are distinct from ideas, it follows that he must also reject Descartes' analysis of judgment as involving the two distinct acts of perceiving and affirming. But it does not follow, as some commentators have thought, that ideas simply are judgments or beliefs.[13] Spinoza clearly maintains that we can have an idea of something's being the case without judging that it is the case—as is shown in the example of the sun (IIp35sch; above, pp. 45 - 46). What he seems to hold is that we judge something to be so if our idea that it is so prevails over other competing ideas (or if there are no competing ideas). Although the conception of ideas as dynamic interacting entities is only developed by Spinoza in the context of his psychology (which forms the subject of the next chapter), it clearly underlies his theory of judgment and belief.

Substance Monism and the Doctrine of Mode

Identity

In chapter 2 we saw that Spinoza's definition of God as "substance consisting of an infinity of attributes, of which each one expresses eternal and infinite essence" presented a critical problem for his monism. Because each attribute is both causally and conceptually independent of all the others, the one substance seemed to be little more than a collection of mutually independent entities. Spinoza did explicitly deny, as we saw, that because two attributes were conceived as "really distinct" or "one without the help of the other" we could therefore conclude that they constituted two substances. And in *Ethics* II he explains the union of mind and body as a special case of a universal relation between modes of the attribute thought and those of extension (IIp7). This relation shows that the one substance is at least a *union*, and not a mere collection, of attributes. Further, this union is necessary, since each of the attributes necessarily exists (Ip19 and dem). This means that it is impossible for substance to be "decomposed" into its attributes, and that is enough to satisfy some commentators on this issue.[14]

But this still does not seem to be a sufficient explanation of the unity of substance. What is the difference between a single substance which consists of a necessary union of attributes, and a necessary union of substances of one attribute? Perhaps the answer is that there is no difference, but Spinoza's claim to have presented a significant metaphysical monism would be stronger if we could find one.[15]

At the other end of the spectrum of solutions to the problem of the plurality of the attributes is that of H.A. Wolfson who takes the attributes to be merely the subjective way the human mind perceives God.[16] I will not dwell on what can be said in favor of this solution, since I think enough can be said against it to rule it out. What is wrong with it is that Spinoza clearly asserts that we have an adequate idea of the attributes (they are among the common notions). To say that we have an adequate idea of something is to say that God has the idea of that thing insofar as he constitutes our mind, and in God all ideas are true. Spinoza also explicitly states that "An infinite intellect comprehends nothing except God's attributes and his affections" (IIp4dem). Overall, he says too much which contradicts the view that the attributes are merely a figment of human subjectivity to seriously entertain it.

Alan Donagan appeared to be on a promising track when he suggested that definitions 4 and 6 of *Ethics* I should be interpreted as asserting not that God's essence consists of an infinity of different essences, but that each diverse attribute fully expresses the one essence

48

of God.[17] A consideration which makes it particularly attractive to think of the attributes as each expressing the same divine essence is that this interpretation offers an explanation of the parallelism of the modes of different attributes, which otherwise appears to be lacking. Spinoza elaborates on the relation between corresponding modes of different attributes in IIp7cor,sch:

> [W}hatever can be perceived by an infinite intellect as constituting an essence of substance pertains to one substance only, and consequently . . . the thinking substance and the extended substance are one and the same substance, which is now comprehended under this attribute, now under that. So also a mode of extension and the idea of that mode are one and the same thing, expressed in two ways. Some of the Hebrews seem to have seen this, as if through a cloud, when they maintained that God, God's intellect and the things understood by Him are one and the same.
>
> For example, a circle existing in nature and the idea of the existing circle, which is also in God, are one and the same thing, which is explained through different attributes. Therefore, whether we conceive nature under the attribute of Extension, or under the attribute of Thought, or under any other attribute, we find one and the same order, or one and the same connection of causes, i.e., that the same things follow one another.

In this passage Spinoza takes parallelism (expressed in the last sentence) to be a consequence of something deeper, namely, *mode identity* (expressed here in the second sentence). That the mind and the body are one and the same thing—a special case of mode identity—is expressed by him at IIp21sch and IIIp2sch.

Recently some commentators have focused on the mode identity thesis, interpreting it in ways which also provide a basis for explaining how each of the conceptually independent attributes can be understood as expressing the same, single divine essence.[18] I shall not elaborate here on their interpretations, but I want to make clear why it is important that ways have been found to make it intelligible how a mode of extension and the idea of that mode can be one and the same thing (numerically identical).

Recall the question we asked above: what would be the difference between a single substance consisting of a necessary union of an infinity of attributes, and a necessary union of an infinity of substances each having one attribute? One difference would seem to lie in the relation between the modes of the substances. That is, if A and B are numerically distinct substances, then the modifications of A and those of B must be numerically distinct. (It seems indisputable that Spinoza would have accepted this principle.) Conversely, if the modifications of substance A and substance B are not numerically distinct—i.e., if they are identical—then A and B are not numerically distinct substances, but they are one and the same substance. In other words, the significance of Spinoza's claim of substance monism lies in numerical mode identity.

Summary

For Descartes, mind and body are two essentially distinct entities, a thinking substance and a certain configuration of accidents (modes) of extension, joined by God in the concrete human being in such a way that they are able to interact causally with one another. For Spinoza who holds that there is only one substance, God, mind and body are modes, of thought and extension, respectively. Since Spinoza denied the possibility of causal interaction between modes of different attributes as unintelligible, he rejected the Cartesian explanation of the union of mind and body. On his own account mind and body are essentially linked as idea and object: the mind is God's idea of an actually existing body. It differs from God's ideas of other bodies as its body differs from others (in complexity, etc.). Spinoza held further that the relation between any mode of any attribute and its idea in God (hence the relation of mind and body) was that of identity. For him all of the mind's cognitive limitations and abilities, including its ability to know the nature of the external world and the essence of God, are explained in terms of the mind's being the idea of the body. Thus, for Spinoza, the mind is not a special creation of God, and knowledge is a natural function, not a supernatural gift.

Spinoza's tendency toward naturalism is also shown in his rejection of Descartes' analysis of judgment and the account he offers in its place. For Descartes to judge that something is the case is to freely affirm or deny an idea. Spinoza, however, denies both the existence of free will (human and divine), and that ideas are separate from volitions or affirmations. On his account to judge that something is the case is for that idea to prevail over others in the mind. Judgment, in other words, is a natural occurrence, not the act of a being which is outside of nature or insulated from natural forces (a thinking substance).

Finally, Spinoza's thesis of mode (mind-body) identity is an integral part of his doctrine of substance monism, and provides the key to understanding the unity of the one substance.

Endnotes

[1] "Synopsis" of the *Meditations*, CSM II, 10; *Meditation* VI, CSM II, 54.

[2] *The Passions of the Soul* I, 8; CSM I, 330.

[3] *The Passions of the Soul* I, 7; CSM I, 330.

[4] *The Passions of the Soul* I, 13; CSM I 333.

[5] *Meditation* VI; CSM II, 56.

[6] *The Passions of the Soul* I, 31; CSM I, 340.

[7] CSM I, 341.

[8] Letters 59 and 60.

[9] *Meditation* III, CSM II, 35.

[10] Lloyd 1996, 97.

[11] Descartes does allow that ideas may be *materially* false. For a discussion of material falsity, see Wilson, 101-120.

[12] In my "Spinoza's Theory of Belief" (unpublished) I show how his doctrine that every idea involves an affirmation appears to be linked to his doctrine that everything strives to persevere in its being. (The latter is discussed below, in chapter 4.)

[13] See Bennett 1984, 162-67; Matson, 67-81.

[14] Curley is one example (1988, 29 – 30).

[15] The French commentator, Martial Gueroult, held that Spinoza's God is a union of one-attribute substances (Gueroult, 232). His explanation of their unity is complicated, but at least partly is based on the necessity of their union. His interpretation is critically discussed in Donagan 1973.

[16] Wolfson I, 148 – 56.

[17] Donagan 1973, 176-77. The same point is made by Joachim, 25; 103.

[18] Bennett 1984, 141-149; Della Rocca 1993; 1996, chs. 6 – 9.

4

Psychology

Introduction

Spinoza's psychology and ethics—his doctrines explaining why human beings think, feel, and act the way they do, and how they should live and interact with each other—are presented in *Ethics* III - V (through Vp20). These doctrines rest on his conception of the mind which is developed in *Ethics* II. According to this conception (a) the mind is the idea of the body; (b) the mind and body are one and the same thing, conceived under different attributes; (c) the mind is a complex system of ideas, just as the body is a complex system of bodies; and (d) the mind has much inadequate and some adequate knowledge of things. The imaginative knowledge it has of itself, the body, external bodies, and finite modes in general, is inadequate; but the common notions or knowledge of the attributes of extension and thought and what can be deduced from them, are adequate.

Spinoza opens *Ethics* III with some critical remarks directed at previous writers who have dealt with human psychology, viz., that they have treated their subject matter as something "outside nature," conceiving of "man in nature as a dominion within a dominion." As a result, they have failed to determine both "the nature and powers of the Affects" or what "the Mind can do to moderate them." Even Descartes, who had the explicit aim of giving a scientific treatment of the emotions, was guilty of this error since he took the will to be exempt from the causal determinism which pervades all physical nature, and concluded that absolute control over the passions was within anyone's capacity.[1] Spinoza asserts his own commitment to naturalism when he writes in the Preface to *Ethics* III that

> [N]ature is always the same, and its virtue and power of acting are everywhere one and the same, i.e., the laws and rules of nature, according to which all things happen, and change from one form to another, are always and everywhere the same. So the way of understanding the nature of anything, of whatever kind, must also be the same, viz., through the universal laws and rules of nature.
>
> The Affects, therefore, of hate, anger, envy, etc., considered in themselves, follow from the same necessity and force of nature as the other singular things.

Consistent with this naturalistic approach, Spinoza's psychology is thoroughly deterministic. As we saw in the last chapter, it is a consequence of Spinoza's general metaphysical doctrine that there is no such thing as freedom of the will. As a finite mode the mind is necessarily determined to exist and act by another finite mode, which in turn is determined by another, and so on ad infinitum (IIp48dem).

At the heart of Spinoza's psychology and ethics are two fundamental concepts: the active/passive distinction and his notion of the *conatus*, or striving of each individual to persevere in its own being. The active/passive distinction is the distinction between being self-determined and being under the control of something external. To suffer a passion or passive emotion is to be under the control of something external. Human virtue and happiness consist in becoming more active or self-determining and less passive. And human interactions are most beneficial to all concerned when the participants are active or self-determining. The endeavor or striving of a thing to persist in its own being both explains why human beings think and act as they do, and provides the basic prescription or "dictate of reason" for what everyone should do, viz., "love himself, seek his own advantage. . . and. . . strive to preserve his own being as far as he can" (IVp18sch).

The Active/Passive Distinction

At the beginning of *Ethics* III, Spinoza distinguishes between what he calls adequate and inadequte causation:

D1: I call that cause adequate whose effect can be clearly and distinctly perceived through it. But I call it partial or inadequate, if its effect cannot be understood through it alone.

Based on this definition he formulates a general notion of action and passion (being acted on):

D2: I say that we act when something happens, in us or outside us, of which we are the adequate cause. . . . I say that we are acted on when something happens in us, or something follows from our nature, of which we are only a partial cause.

As we have already seen Spinoza denies that there can be any interaction between body and mind; hence passive mental states cannot be caused by any bodily states or events (IIp6, IIIp2). But since "the Mind and the Body are one and the same thing," it follows that "the order of actions and passions of our Body is, by nature, at one with the order of actions and passions of the Mind" (IIIp2sch).

Spinoza maintains in IIIp1 and p3 that insofar as the mind has adequate ideas it acts and insofar as it has inadequate ideas it is passive. This is because when an idea is adequate in the mind, God has that idea or is the cause of that idea insofar as he constitutes the mind. In general, the cause of an idea of x is the idea of the cause of x (by the parallelism of modes of thought and extension). Those things of which the human mind has adequate ideas are things the ideas of whose causes are also in the human mind, i.e., things which are "common to all" and "equally present in the part and in the whole." These include the attributes and whatever follows from the attributes (the infinite modes). Because an attribute is conceived through itself or has no further cause through which it must be understood, the idea of an attribute (and consequently, of whatever follows from an attribute) must be adequate in every mind. By contrast, when the mind has an inadequate idea of a thing, the idea of the cause of the thing is beyond the reach of the mind. That is, God does not have the idea of the cause of the thing insofar as he constitutes the mind. Therefore, since the idea of the cause of the thing is the cause of the idea of the thing, the mind itself is not (does not contain) the cause of its idea.

For Spinoza the passions proper, or passive emotions, are simply a subclass of inadequate idea. But he also maintains that there are active emotions, ones which we have in virtue of our capacity to form adequate ideas. Minimizing the former and maximizing the latter is a goal of rational behavior.

The *Conatus* or Striving to Persist

Spinoza's doctrine of the *conatus* or striving to persist, is expressed in IIIp4 -p9. Its core is constituted by propositions 6 and 7, which are as follows:

P6: Each thing, as far as it can by its own power, strives to persevere in its being.

P7: The striving by which each thing strives to persevere in its being is nothing but the actual essence of the thing.

A fundamental question concerning this doctrine is whether or not the striving which these propositions attribute to things should be interpreted teleologically. A teleological interpretation would construe these propositions as asserting that each thing aims at its own self-preservation, or that the goal of continuing in existence is a fundamental and irreducible factor in explaining the behavior of things. Such an interpretation need not hold that individuals are necessarily conscious of this goal or tendency, that they consciously aim at self-preservation. A nonteleological interpretation would construe the *conatus* doctrine as asserting merely that each thing has a certain nature which is a determining factor in whatever happens to it, and which, if the thing were left to itself (not interfered with, or affected by anything external), would determine that the thing continue indefinitely in a certain way. Viewed in this way, the principle that each thing strives to continue in its being would be a generalization of the principle of inertia, which Spinoza expresses as "a body in motion moves until it is determined by another body to rest; and . . . a body at rest also remains at rest until it is determined to motion by another" (lemma 3cor, following IIp13).

Elsewhere in the *Ethics* Spinoza explicitly rejects teleological explanations or explanations of happenings in terms of a goal or purpose or aim. He uses the term "final cause" to refer to a purpose or aim taken as having explanatory power, and writes in I Appendix that

Nature has no end set before it, and . . . all final causes are nothing but human fictions. . . . [A]ll things proceed by a certain eternal necessity of nature, and with the greatest perfection.

. . . [T]his doctrine concerning the end turns nature completely upside down. For what is really a cause, it considers as an effect, and conversely. . . . What is by nature prior it makes posterior. (I Appendix; see also IV Preface.)

Another important point in support of the nonteleological interpretation of the striving to persist is that there is nothing in the demonstrations of IIIp4-9 which requires or supports a teleological interpretation. In fact, the demonstration of IIIp7 (and the proposition itself) strongly suggests otherwise:

> From the given essence of each thing some things necessarily follow (by IP36), and things are able [to produce] nothing but what follows necessarily from their determinate nature (by Ip29). So the power of each thing, or the striving by which it (either alone or with others) does anything, or strives to do anything—i.e., (by P6), the power, or striving, by which it strives to persevere in its being, is nothing but the given or actual essence of the thing itself, q.e.d.

This passage seems to say that what explains what a thing does alone or how it interacts with other things, is the thing's essence—its fundamental nature. And that seems to be quite different from saying that the goal of continuing in existence explains what the thing does.

By contrast, the use Spinoza makes of his *conatus* doctrine in his psychology strongly supports a teleological interpretation of the notion of striving. This is particularly evident in the use he makes of the doctrine to derive IIIp12 and p13, which are fundamental to his entire psychology. Proposition 12 states that "The mind, as far as it can, strives to imagine those things that increase or aid the Body's power of acting." Spinoza proves this proposition by first pointing out that when the mind imagines things which increase the body's power of acting, the body is in fact affected in a way in which its power of acting is increased; hence the mind's power of acting must also be increased. He then argues simply that "Therefore (byP6 or P9) the mind, as far as it can, strives to imagine those things, q.e.d." The demonstration of IIIp13, that "When the Mind imagines those things that diminish or restrain the Body's power of acting, it strives, as far as it can, to recollect things that exclude their existence," is similar. In it Spinoza reasons simply that since the mind's own power of acting is diminished as long as it imagines a thing which diminishes the body's power of acting, and since the mind continues to imagine a thing until it imagines something else which excludes the thing's existence, it follows that the mind will strive, as far as it can, to imagine or recollect what will exclude the thing's existence. Clearly, in both these propositions, the mind's increasing or retaining undiminished its own power of acting is invoked as a goal to explain the direction of thought.

This teleological use of the principle of the *conatus* or striving appears to be inconsistent not only with Spinoza's rejection of teleological explanations and final causes, but also with his commitment to the naturalistic premise that we must understand everything in nature in the same general kind of way. There is no evidence that Spinoza thinks that there is room for teleological explanations in physics. The movements of a body are to be explained purely in terms of efficient causation, i.e., in terms of the forces acting on that body, not in terms of any goal sought by it. (In this respect the basically Cartesian physics of Spinoza differs from that of Aristotle who held that different kinds of bodies have a natural tendency to move to the center or periphery of the universe.) How then can there be such explanations in psychology or the human sciences in general?

The only way I can think of to reconcile Spinoza's rejection of teleology, his commitment to the view that all things can be explained in the same general kinds of ways, and his teleological use of the principal of striving is that he regards a teleological principle of striving as a kind of stopgap explanation of the behavior of many things until we have a better understanding of the efficient causes which determine their behavior. In other words, he holds that in principle, any teleological explanation—any explanation in terms of the aims or goals of the subject, including the airm of persevering in its own being—can be replaced by one in terms of efficient causation.

Consider for a moment what is involved in the behavior of complex individuals when they appear to be acting for the goal of self-preservation, or where their actions appear to be explainable in terms of a tendency toward self-preservation. Behavior appears to be most obviously oriented toward this goal when an individual does something adaptive in response to an environmental change. For example, when the environment turns colder, the blood vessels close to the skin in a warm-blooded animal contract, with the result that less heat is lost and body temperature is maintained. Under conditions of scarce food supply or near starvation, the metabolic rate of an animal decreases, so less fuel is burned and body weight is maintained. We know that many such adaptive behaviors are explainable in terms of "feedback" mechanisms, that the body of a warm blooded animal, for instance, has a biological thermostatic mechanism which functions analogously to that of the thermostat on a furnace. It is not implausible to believe that all such adaptive behaviors can be similarly explained. Clearly, having a sizable repertoire of such adaptive behaviors enables a complex individual to endure and preserve its being just as though it were ultimately governed by the tendency or goal of self-preservation.

Thus, to say an individual "strives to persevere in its being" may be taken to mean simply that an individual has some feedback mechanisms which enable it to respond adaptively to its environment. Such mechanisms and responses can include ones which are preemptive, such as storing fat when food is plentiful, or other activities under "friendly" conditions which result in an increased capacity to adapt to and endure hostile ones. Spinoza need have no more than this in mind when he reasons from the fact that "Each thing, as far as it can by its own power, strives to persevere in its being" to "The Mind, as far as it can, strives to imagine those things that increase or aid the Body's power of acting."

The Passive Emotions (Passions)

Spinoza offers the following definition of an affect or emotion:

> D3: By affect I understand affections of the Body by which the Body's power of acting is increased or diminished, aided or restrained, and at the same time, the ideas of these affections.

He then adds in explanation:

> Therefore, if we can be the adequate cause of any of these affections, I understand by the Affect an action; otherwise, a passion.

Spinoza speaks of the emotions both as they relate to the mind alone, and as they relate to mind and body. By the identity of mind and body, the idea of a bodily state which involves a transition to greater or lesser power of acting will itself constitute the mind's transition to a greater or lesser power of acting (IIIp11). Considered in relation to the mind alone, the passions proper, or passive emotions, are ideas of passive states of the body which involve a change in the body's power of acting. As such, they are a subclass of imaginative ideas (ideas of the affections of the body caused by external bodies), hence are necessrily inadequate or confused (IIp28).

Spinoza recognizes three primary affects in terms of which all the others can be understood or analyzed. Joy is the passion by which the mind passes to a greater perfection; sadness that by which it passes to a lesser one (IIIp11sch). What Spinoza identifies as the third of the primary affects, desire, is in fact not covered by the official definition of "affect" (IIIdfn3, above), although in the "General Definition of the Affects" (given at the end of *Ethics* III) Spinoza adds a somewhat awkward clause to cover desire.[2]   In a general sense desire is simply the striving for self preservation (IIIp9sch; "Definitions of the Affects I"). For a person to have a particular desire is for the person to be determined to act in a certain way; and for the mind to have a particular desire is for it to be determined to think certain thoughts (III, "Definitions of the Affects I"; "General Definition of the Affects"). The principle of striving (IIIp6) implies that in general we will seek or desire to obtain joy and avoid or minimize sadness (IIIp 12, 13, 25, 26, 28, 29, 54).

All other emotions are either varieties of joy, sadness, or desire, or combinations of these. Thus, love is joy accompanied by the idea of an external cause; hatred is sadness accompanied by the idea of an external cause; and jealousy is a vacillation of mind between love and hate (IIIp13cor,sch; p35sch).

The passive emotions can be aroused directly by our body or a part of it being affected by something which itself causes it to undergo some transition in its power of acting; or indirectly, through the association of ideas (IIIp14). Through association anything can become a source of pleasure or pain or an object of desire (IIIp15); we can feel love or hatred for things for no other reason than because they resemble or otherwise remind us of other things which we love or hate (IIIp15, 15sch., 16). The passive emotions can also be aroused by "sympathy" or our becoming aware of someone like ourselves who is experiencing some emotion. Sharing or imitating someone's sadness in this way is pity; sharing or imitating their desire is emulation. The imitation of a person's love for what she alone can possess leads to a desire to possess that thing which being frustrated leads to envy, a species of hatred (sadness) caused by another's good fortune (III, "Definitions of the Affects" XXIII).

In addition to the passive emotions, there are emotions which are related to us insofar as we act. "When the mind considers itself and its power of acting it rejoices" (IIIp53). Since insofar as it has adequate ideas it does necessarily consider itself and its power of acting, adequate thinking (thinking in which we are the cause of our own ideas) involves joy. Further, since our striving to persevere in our own being is expressed both in adequate and inadequate ideas (IIIp9), and since this striving is desire, desire can be active as well as passive. But there are no active emotions of sadness, since by Spinoza's *conatus* doctrine, we cannot be the cause of our own sadness (transition to a lower level of activity).

The Strength of the Passions

One of Spinoza's aims in *Ethics* III and IV is to give an account of the "nature and strength" of the passions, with a view toward determining how we can control them, and to what degree. What is bad about the passions is that in so far as we are subject to them, we are "driven about in many ways by external causes, and that, like waves on the sea, driven by contrary winds, we toss about, not knowing our outcome and our fate" (IIIp59sch). Because we are finite modes, or part of Nature, it is inevitable that we are acted on or passive; and because for every finite thing in nature, there is another which is more powerful, or by which the first can be destroyed, it follows that our power is infinitely surpassed by the power of external things (IVax1, p2-p4).

Spinoza's doctrine of the force or strength of the passions rests ultimately on his conception of ideas as dynamic entities, and a semi-implicit theory of force relations among them. Every idea is an individual modification of thought, hence every idea has itself a certain force of existing or strives to persevere in its being. The passions of joy and sadness (and all their varieties) are a subclass of imaginative ideas, viz., those whose objects are modifications of the body which involve a transition in the body's power of activity. Because a passion is the idea of a bodily modification, its strength is proportionate to that of the bodily modification, and like that of the bodily modification, is partly derived from and partly depends on its external cause (IVp5). For this reason any emotion may be beyond our control (IVp6). Further, as an imaginative idea, a passion will persist as long as the bodily modification persists (IIp17cor) and it will be able to be restrained or removed only by the idea of a bodily modification which involves the opposite transition, i.e., an opposite affect (Ivp7). Whether it is restrained or destroyed will depend on the relative strength of the two affects. Although Spinoza's account of the strength of the passions focuses on their external causes, we ourselves are a cause of the strength and persistence of joyful passions, insofar as by our nature we seek to be affected with joy. Spinoza recognizes this when he notes that a desire that arises from joy "must be defined both by human power and the power of the external cause" (IVp18dem).

As an imaginative idea an emotion is strengthened by other ideas which posit the existence of its object and restrained by other ideas which exclude its object's existence. Thus our emotions toward things which we imagine as present are stronger than those toward things which we imagine as future or past and not present, since to imagine a thing as not present is to imagine it along with something that excludes its existence. Similarly our emotions toward things which are not present but which are imagined as nearer in time—e.g., in the recent past—are stronger than those toward things which are more removed from the present, since to imagine a thing as nearer in time is to imagine things which exclude its existence less than if it is imagined as temporally more distant (IVp9 and dem and sch; .p10 and dem and sch). Modality affects our imagination of things, and hence our emotions toward them, in a way similar to time. Thus, an emotion toward a thing we imagine as necessary is (other things being equal) stronger than one which we imagine as possible or contingent, since to imagine something as necessary is to affirm its existence, but to imagine it as merely possible or contingent is to imagine what excludes its present existence (IVp11-p13).

Controlling the Passive Emotions

Spinoza remarks in the Preface to *Ethics* V, that

> because the power of the Mind is defined only by understanding, as I have shown above, we shall determine, by the Mind's knowledge alone, the remedies for the affects.

There is one obvious sense in which control of the passions depends on knowledge, viz., we need true judgments concerning what is good and bad to guide our actions. But since the force of an idea is not a function of its truth, such judgments have no power to move us and no power against the passions insofar as they are true (IVp1sch; p14). Only insofar as such judgments are themselves affects (ideas of a transition in the body's power of acting) are they able to exercise a restraining force on emotions which are opposed to them (IVp8, 14).

Descartes agrees with Spinoza that true judgments are necessary but, in themselves, insufficient "weapons" against the passions. What is needed rather are "firm and determinate judgments bearing upon the knowledge of good and evil, which the soul has resolved to follow in guiding its conduct."[3] What is needed, in other words, are judgments backed up by the power of the will.

Descartes defines the passions as "those perceptions, sensations or emotions of the soul which we refer particularly to it, and which are caused, maintained and strengthened by some movement of the spirits."[4] By the "spirits" Descartes means what he calls the "animal spirits," a rarified bodily fluid which circulates throughout the brain, nervous system and muscles (see above, p.). When he says the passions are referred to the soul he means that we feel them as being in the soul (in contrast to e.g., hunger, which is referred to the body, and heat which is referred to some external body). He notes that as perceptions, the passions are obscure and confused; and that they are better called "emotions" on account of their ability to agitate and disturb the soul.[5]

Descartes does not hold that we have direct, voluntary control over the passions because the passions are a type of perception, and in general, we do not have direct control over whether we will perceive a thing or not. Thus, just as I cannot prevent my hearing a loud noise merely by willing not to hear it, so I cannot prevent my feeling a surge of anger or fear merely by willing not to feel it. We do, however, have direct voluntary control over our bodily movements such as striking or running; hence we are generally able, by an act of will, to prevent the movements of the body which accompany a passion, or to interrupt the natural sequence of physical events which occurs in cases of anger and fear.[6] (The physical manifestations of a passion are not caused by the passion, but on Descartes' account, are simply a reflex response to the same physical stimulus which also sets in motion the chain of events that results in the passion.) We also have a kind of indirect voluntary control over the passions insofar as we have the ability to alter the natural or learned sequences of events which result in our feeling some emotion. Descartes appears to think that we can do this either by breaking a connection between certain movements of the pineal gland and certain thoughts in the mind; or by breaking a connection between different movements of the pineal gland and animal spirits. In other words, we can recondition or train ourselves to feel courage instead of fear when we see a dangerous animal or shared pleasure instead of envy when we hear about a colleague's success. Descartes is somewhat vague about the mechanism by which new emotional response patterns are created, but he evidently thinks there is no limit to our ability to create them. He writes

> For since we are able, with a little effort, to change the movements of the brain in animals devoid of reason, it is evident that we can do so still more effectively in the case of men. Even those who have the weakest souls could acquire absolute mastery over all their passions if we employed sufficient ingenuity in training and guiding them.[7]

But even on Descartes' own theory of mind and body, it is implausible to hold that the mind can have such absolute or unlimited control of its passions. Granted that the will is free, the body is still, as Spinoza would put it, a part of nature, and the mind, insofar as it perceives, is subject to the effects of extended nature. Hence the body. and the mind insofar as it is subject to being affected by the body, may resist our best attempts to reprogram their responses. Spinoza had this in mind when he remarked in criticism of Descartes,

> [N]or do I know whether the motions of the Passions which we have joined closely to firm judgments can be separated from them again by corporeal causes. If so, it would follow that although the Mind had firmly resolved to face dangers, and had joined the motions of daring to this decision, nevertheless, once the danger had been seen, the gland might be so suspended that the Mind could think only of flight (V Preface).

Nevertheless, Spinoza is in agreement with Descartes in holding that the ability to create new patterns of emotional response is an important part of the control we have over our emotions, although this ability is not unlimited or absolute. When the mind is not in a state of emotional agitation it is able to order and connect the affections of the body "according to the order of the intellect." For example,

> By this power of rightly ordering and connecting the affections of the Body, we can bring it about that we are not easily affected with evil affects. . . .

> For example, we have laid it down as a maxim of life . . . that Hate is to be conquered by Love, *or* Nobility, not by repaying it with Hate in return. But in order that we may always have this rule of reason ready when it is needed, we ought to think about and meditate frequently on the common wrongs of men, and how they may be warded off best by Nobility. For if we join the image of a wrong to the imagination of this maxim, it will always be ready for us(by IIP18) when a wrong is done to us (Vp10sch).

The differences between Spinoza and Descartes, however, go beyond disagreement over whether or not we can have absolute mastery over our passions. For Descartes, the source of our power over the passions lies in the will. By the strength of our will we reprogram our brains and the mind-body connection in the way our intellect judges to be the best. For Spinoza "will and intellect are one and the same" (IIp49cor), and the source of the mind's power lies in knowledge. Reprograming our emotional responses is more than just replacing "bad" responses with "good" ones. It involves developing and restructuring our mind or mental life in such a way that our thoughts and emotions become more determined from within and less determined by external causes.

In both our cognitive and our emotional lives, the strength or power of the mind is manifest in adequate thinking (IIIp1,3; IVdfn8). In adequate thinking the mind itself is the cause of both its affective or emotional and non-affective or cognitive states, although these cannot be separated, since insofar as the mind thinks adequately it experiences joy (IIIp58). A strong mind is one whose thought is generally, or to a greater extent, governed by its adequate ideas. Such a mind may have as many inadequate ideas as any other, but these play a lesser role or are even insignificant in determining the direction of its thought. Spinoza's example of our two ideas of the sun can be used to illustrate this (IIp35sch; IVp1sch; above, pp. 45 - 46). What we know fully adequately is only the common notions and what follows necessarily from the common notions—extension and the infinite eternal modes of extension. Such knowledge finds expression in the most basic laws of physical science. No idea of the sun's actual distance can be fully adequate for the same reason that no knowledge of the actual properties of individual finite things can be fully adequate. The ideas of the causes of such things are beyond the reach of the human mind. But the idea of the sun as "more than 600 diameters of the earth away from us" fits into a theory about how things are, whose framework is provided by the common notions, better than the purely imaginative idea of it as about two hundred feet away. Thus, the idea of the sun as more than 600 diameters of the earth away from us derives more support from the common notions than the idea of it as about 200 feet away. Although the latter does not disappear (since it is reinforced by immediate experience), it is the former which plays a significant role in our thinking about the sun. A mind whose conception of the world is predominantly formed by ideas which are connected "according to the order of the intellect" is cognitively strong.

Such a mind, however, will also be emotionally strong, since it will deal with its passions in the same manner it deals with the "illusions" of sense. "Illusion" is a poor word to describe an idea such as that of the sun as being about 200 feet away, since this idea is not about or indicative of nothing real. Rather it is a highly confused idea of a modification of our body which is caused by the sun. When we form a broad conception of things which includes an idea of the sun's actual distance and a conception of how the senses work and how the modification of the body is caused by the sun, and whose framework is provided by the common notions, then the idea of the sun as about 200 feet away becomes relatively weak in our minds.

Like our original idea of the sun, the passive emotions are confused or inadequate ideas. Through fitting them into a broader conception of things which is framed by the common notions, and within which we understand both their nature as ideas of modifications of our body and the nature of their objects, we weaken their relative force. Consider, for example, my anger at (hatred of) a friend who has betrayed a confidence. To the extent that I understand the causes of her action I view it as necessitated, and my hatred is thereby diminished (Vp6). And to the extent that I understand my emotion for what it is, viz., a kind of sadness or idea of my body's transition to a lower level of activity, I distinguish or separate the emotion from its object—my friend and her action. Thus I cease to project something which is only in me—sadness—on to the world as an objective quality of a thing—evil. (This is analogous to separating what is merely a feature of a modification of one's body from what is really a property of the sun.) Insofar as I am able to make such a detachment of my sadness from its object, I destroy the emotion of hatred (sadness accompanied by the idea of an external cause), and thus remove one obstacle which would prevent me from dealing in a rational way with the sadness of having a friend betray a confidence. Thus, insofar as a passion is better understood—i.e., insofar as we are able to relate it to the basic conceptual framework provided by the common notions—it ceases to be a passion. Although we can never rid ourselves of passions or ensure that we will never be overcome, through knowledge or adequate ideas we put ourselves more in charge of our emotions and render them less effective.

Summary

Spinoza's doctrine of the *conatus* or striving of a thing to persevere in its being is a fundamental principle of his psychology. The use Spinoza makes of this principle clearly indicates that it is teleological in nature, i.e., to invoke the principle is to explain a thing's behavior in terms of the goal of increasing or maintaining its power of activity. But such a teleological principle would be in conflict with Spinoza's general rejection of teleology and with his dual commitment to naturalism and explanation in terms of efficient causation in physics. I suggested, therefore, that for Spinoza the principle of striving is not an ultimate one, but that in principle, any explanation of a thing's behavior in terms of the goal of maintaining or increasing its power of activity could be replaced with one in terms of efficient causation. How this can be the case can be understood by considering the way in which "feedback" mechanisms work to enable complex organisms to respond adaptively to their environment.

Spinoza distinguishes three basic affects or emotions: joy, sadness and desire. Joy and sadness are simply ideas of the body's transition to a greater and lesser power of activity, respectively. Desire in the general sense is the mind's striving to persevere in its being; specific desires are its determinations to specific kinds of thoughts, e.g., to desire a house is to be determined to think about the advantages of a house. The passions proper, or passive emotions, are ones of which we ourselves are not the adequate (complete) cause. The passive emotions of joy and sadness (and all their varieties) are nothing but inadequate ideas of bodily states which involve a transition to a greater or lesser power of activity. And passive desires are ones in which we are determined by something other than ourselves.

Thus, to be subject to the passions is to be subject to the control of things outside us. And, insofar as we are finite parts of nature, it is inevitable that we suffer passions. It is also inevitable that at times we be overcome by a passion, since the strength of a passion is partially dependent on that of its external cause, and our strength is infinitely surpassed by that of things outside us.

For Spinoza, the source of our strength against the passions lies in knowledge, not, as for Descartes, the will. Like the illusions of sense, the passions are simply inadequate ideas of the body's modifications. Our power is expressed in adequate thinking. To the degree that we are able to understand our imaginative ideas which are errors or illusions, and place them within a conceptual framework which is based on the common notions of extension and thought, they cease to be illusory, although they do not disappear. Similarly, to the degree that we understand the passive emotions and fit them into the order of the intellect, they too lose their power to compel us.

Endnotes

[1] *The Passions of the Soul* I, 41, 50; CSM I, 343, 348.

[2] The "General Definition of the Affects" is "An Affect that is called a Passion of the mind is a confused idea, by which the Mind affirms of its Body, or of some part of it, a greater or lesser force of existing than before, which, when it is given, determines the Mind to think of this rather than that."

[3] *The Passions of the Soul* I, 48; CSM I, 347.

[4] *The Passions of the Soul* I, 27; CSM I, 338-39.

[5] *The Passions of he Soul* I, 28; CSM I, 339.

[6] *The Passions of the Soul* I, 46; CSM I, 345.

[7] *The Passions of the Soul* I, 50; CSM I, 348.

5

Ethical Doctrine

The metaphysics, theory of knowledge and psychology of *Ethics* I-IVp18 provide the framework within which Spinoza develops his ethical doctrine. Insofar as it involves notions of the good, happiness, virtue, and what we *should* do or how we *should* act, Spinoza's ethics is not strictly deducible from these doctrines. Rather, they provide the base on which Spinoza constructs his ethics by adding to them (1) naturalistic definitions of "good," "evil" and "virtue;" and (2) the prescriptive premise that (reason dictates that) everyone should pursue his own advantage or strive as far as he can to persevere in his own being.

Spinoza's Ethical Naturalism

Spinoza's analysis of value terms in general is completely naturalistic. In other words, for him, all such terms are able to be replaced without loss of meaning, with ones which are purely descriptive. Thus, "good," "evil," "beautiful," "ugly," and others "indicate nothing positive in things, considered in themselves," but rather are descriptive of how we or our imagination is affected by things (IV Preface; I Appendix). What is advantageous to us, or preserves our being, or is a source of joy or pleasure, or satisfies some desire is said to be good; what is disadvantageous, etc., is said to be evil. Thus, "we neither strive for, nor will, neither want, nor desire anything because we judge it to be good; on the contrary, we judge something to be good because we strive for it, will it, want it, and desire it" (IIIp9sch). "Good" and "evil" are thus generally relative to the individual. Because individual human beings differ with respect to what affects them with joy or pleasure and have different desires, what is good to one may be indifferent or bad to another (IV Preface; IIIp51 and sch). Only in a civil state is there common agreement as to what is good and evil (IVp37sch2). In *Ethics* III Spinoza writes that each person judges what is good and what is bad "from his own affect" (p39sch, p51sch), but in *Ethics* IVp8 he identifies the judgment that a thing is good or evil with the affect or emotion (of joy or sadness) itself. This is because to judge that a thing is good or evil is simply to be aware of joy or sadness, i.e., to have an idea of joy or sadness. Hence, by the identity of idea and object, to judge that a thing is good or bad just is to be affected with an emotion. The importance of this identification is that for Spinoza value judgments have affective force. To judge that something is good (evil) is to be moved to seek (avoid) it. The "strength" of any such judgment is independent of its truth or falsity, and can be outweighed by countervailing passions, particularly when the judgment concerns things in general (or future or contingent things) and the passion is fueled by a present object (IVp14-17).

Noncognitivism is the view that value judgments do not express facts, or are not susceptible of being true or false. In general, philosophers who identify moral judgments with (expressions of) emotion—"emotivists"—are noncognitivists. But this is not the case with Spinoza, since he rejects the more basic distinction between judgment and emotion on which the cognitivist/noncognitivist distinction rests. The emotions for Spinoza are a subclass of ideas, and a prevailing idea is a judgment. Value judgments generally express only a fact about the subject, but they are factual, nonetheless.

Spinoza's analysis of virtue is similarly naturalistic: "By virtue and power I understand the same thing, i.e., (IIIP7), virtue, in so far as it is related to man, is the very essence or nature of man, in so far as he has the power of bringing about certain things, which can be understood through the laws of his nature alone" (IVdfn8). Spinoza's notion of virtue appears to be related to the ancient conception of virtue as excellence. Like that concept, it is applicable to non-human individuals as well as to humans, and is not a specifically moral concept.

Spinoza's commitment to ethical naturalism is also shown in his "derivation" of the basic ethical doctrine that everyone should pursue her own advantage. In this regard he writes

> Since reason demands nothing contrary to nature, it demands
> that everyone love himself, seek his own advantage, what is
> really useful to him, want what will really lead man to a

greater perfection, and absolutely, that everyone should strive to preserve his own being as far as he can (IVp18sch).

Although Spinoza speaks of the "dictates of reason," on his account ethics reduces to psychology. Knowledge of human good is simply a matter of knowing what human beings are; and the "guidance of reason" is the guidance which adequate knowledge of human nature provides.

Some Initial Difficulties

There are two problems, which seem to arise at the outset, for Spinoza's propounding any sort of ethical doctrine. One has to do with his determinism. If human beings are, like everything else in nature, completely necessitated in all that they think and do, what point is there in trying to educate them regarding how they should live? The answer to this is that although every person is completely determined in her actions, being introduced to new ideas regarding how one should live can itself be a determining factor in her subsequent behavior. In fact, if determinism were false, or if, in particular, education, information and new ideas had no tendency whatsoever to influence people or be a factor in determining their behavior, then it would make no sense to write treatises with the intention of demonstrating to them how they should live. If teaching and education are to make a difference, determinism must be true.

The second problem has to do with Spinoza's analysis of value terms, and is a bit more complicated. If good is not a property of things, and what is good is relative to the individual's desires, how can Spinoza claim to offer a general prescription regarding how a person should live? Spinoza's response to this potential objection would be to acknowledge that insofar as human beings are subject to passions, almost anything can be an object of desire, hence anything can be a good. But insofar as a person is under the influence of a passion she is determined by external causes, not by her own nature alone. What is truly good for a person is what she strives for from her own nature alone, what satisfies her active desires. He also holds, however, that human beings differ in their affects as much as they differ in their nature or essence (IIIp57). Insofar therefore, as he is offering a general prescription regarding what is good for all human beings, Spinoza must assume that there is some common human nature which all humans share, or that all human beings are at least sufficiently similar that his general prescriptions make sense. Based on this general conception of human nature (which I discuss at more length below, pp. 76 - 78), what Spinoza aims to provide with his ethical doctrine is knowledge regarding human good. Such a good is relative to human nature, in the sense that what is advantageous or pleasurable to human beings is not necessarily so to horses or dolphins, but it is absolute (invariant) with respect to individual human beings insofar as it is a function of human nature or desire.

The Ethical Doctrine

To contemporary readers one of the most striking aspects of Spinoza's ethical doctrine is that it is primarily concerned with the question of how a person should live and the personal traits she should cultivate, rather than with questions of right and wrong and our obligations to others. Perhaps a sufficient explanation for this is his naturalism—outside of a civil society there are no obligations to others, and no right and wrong. In any case, in this respect too he is more akin to classical writers (Plato, Aristotle, the Stoics) than to modern ones.

Our most fundamental desire is to preserve our being or to live (IVp21). To the extent to which we are self-determining or do what follows from our nature alone, we necessarily do what preserves our being (IIIp4). Virtue is the power to do what follows from our nature alone, to be self-determining (IVdfn8). Since there is nothing beyond themselves for whose sake individuals strive to preserve themselves, self-determination or virtue is an end in itself (IVp18sch; p25). We are self-determined only insofar as we have adequate ideas (IIIp1,p3). Hence, we act from virtue only insofar as we understand or are determined by adequate ideas; and ultimately we seek no end other than understanding. Thus,

> [T]hings are good only insofar as they aid man to enjoy the life of the Mind, which is defined by understanding. On the other hand, those that prevent man from being able to perfect his reason and enjoy the rational life, those only we say are evil (IV Appendix, v).

Since God is an absolutely infinite being, and without God nothing else can be known, knowledge of God is both our greatest good—most advantageous to us—and our greatest virtue—the source of our power (IVp28).

We are, however, finite modes, and thus necessarily subject to the effects of things outside us and dependent on them. For a person to be completely free, or self-determining, is an unattainable ideal, although it is the model which guides Spinoza's practical doctrine (IV Preface; p67-

73). Part of his doctrine is negative, educating us with respect to the real harm or evil involved in the pursuit and possession of many apparent goods and virtues. Thus, while joy is always directly or in itself good (since it is an increase in our power of acting), and sadness is always directly or in itself bad (since it is a decrease in our power of acting), joy can be excessive and evil. It is so when, as a bodily affect it primarily increases the power of acting only of one part of the body, thus disrupting the body's equilibrium and rendering it less able to affect, and be affected by, other bodies (IVp38, 41, 43, 44). When this happens, the mind is less able to think and perceive, so such joy is actually harmful. Typically, on Spinoza's view, the passions are excessive, even to the point of madness:

> [T]he affects by which we are daily torn are generally related to a part of the Body which is affected more than the others. Generally, then, the affects are excessive, and occupy the Mind in the consideration of only one object so much that it cannot think of others. . . . [W]e sometimes see that men are so affected by one object that, although it is not present, they still believe they have it with them.
>
> When this happens to a man who is not asleep, we say that he is mad or insane. Nor are they thought to be less mad who burn with Love, and dream, both night and day, only of a lover or a courtesan. . . . But when a greedy man thinks of nothing else but profit, or money, and an ambitious man of esteem, they are not thought to be mad, because they are usually troublesome and are considered worthy of Hate. But Greed, Ambition, and Lust really are species of madness, event though they are not numbered among the diseases (IVp44sch).

In a similar vein, humility and repentance, two emotions ordinarily commended as virtues, are really species of sadness (sadness which comes from considering our own lack of power, and sadness which is accompanied by the idea of something we believe we have done, respectively—III Definitions of the Affects, xxvi, xxvii). Thus, in themselves, they are evil, not good and not virtues, although they may be useful in restraining excessive emotions, especially ones which are antisocial. Spinoza observes:

> The mob is terrifying, if unafraid. So it is no wonder that the Prophets, who considered the common advantage, not that of the few, commended Humility, Repentance, and Reverence so greatly (IVp54sch).

Most desires which spring from the passive affects are blind in that they have no regard for what would be good for the whole individual; all are blind in that they take no account of the long run, or whether their satisfaction will cause the individual to suffer some greater evil or lose some greater good (IVp58schl., p60 and sch). The most innocent, purest, and greatest passive joys have the potential to be bad or harmful—to our disadvantage—when everything is taken into account. For this reason we should strive to become the active generators of our desires.

We actively generate our own desires to the extent that they spring from or are governed by our adequate knowledge. Adequate thinking itself is affective because insofar as the mind thinks adequately it experiences joy, and the more it understands, the more it desires to understand. Further, insofar as a person has an adequate understanding of himself as a finite mode of thought identical with a certain finite mode of extension, i.e., as embodied, he understands that he has bodily needs that must be satisfied in order that his mind be capable of understanding, and that bodily pleasures which involve an increase in the power of acting of the body as a whole are necessarily accompanied by an increase in the mind's power to think. Therefore,

> To use things. . . and take pleasure in them as far as possible—not, of course, to the point where we are disgusted with them, for there is no pleasure in that—this is the part of a wise man.

> It is the part of a wise man, I say, to refresh and restore himself in moderation with pleasant food and drink, with scents, with the beauty of green plants, with decoration, music, sports, the theater, and other things of this kind, which anyone can use without injury to another. For the human Body is composed of a great many parts of different natures, which constantly require new and varied nourishment, so that the whole Body may be equally capable of all the things which can follow from its nature, and hence, so that the Mind also may be equally capable of understanding many things (IVp45cor2sch).

To experience an emotion or do something which in fact is conducive to our real advantage is to experience or do what agrees with reason; to be determined by our adequate knowledge of ourselves to experience or do it is to experience or do it from reason. We are genuinely best off when we act from reason because only reason has regard to the whole person and for the long run. In any given circumstance a person may do the same thing under the influence of a passive emotion as he would do if he were determined by reason. Under the influence of pity (sadness generated in us by another's suffering), for example, a person may be moved to help someone, just as he would desire to do if he were determined through reason alone. But only reason is a reliable guide to action. That is, only when we act from reason do we do what we know for certain is good (IVp50dem; p50cor,sch).

While those passive emotions which are conducive to our real advantage agree with reason, others are always opposed to it. These include all those which essentially involve ignorance—pride and despondency, overestimation and scorn. One cannot be proud or despondent without misestimating one's own power; and one cannot overestimate another person or be scornful of her without ignorance of her nature. In general affects of sadness and the desires which arise from them, e.g., hope and fear, are not always opposed to reason, since they may be useful in curbing excessive or harmful pleasures (fear of consequences may prevent us from doing something pleasant but foolish), but insofar as we are guided by reason these passive affects serve no necessary function. Reason alone determines us to choose a lesser present evil over a greater future one. This difference between acting from fear, which is a passion, and acting from reason, is important because the person who acts out of fear is motivated by sadness, while the person who acts from reason is motivated by joy. And the latter is stronger since desires which spring from joy are, other things being equal, stronger than those which spring from sadness, since the former derive their strength from ourselves and an external cause, whereas the strength of the latter depends on us alone. The person who is guided by reason is stronger than she who is moved only by a desire that springs from sadness, partly because the former is able to harness the natural forces of her passive emotions in the service of her own genuine advantage, much as technology harnesses—but does not create—the forces of physical nature.

Interpersonal Ethics

Spinoza's ethical doctrine appears to be unequivocally egoistic.[1] Reason demands that "everyone love himself, seek his own advantage, . . . [and] strive to preserve his own being as far as he can" (IVp18sch). The foundation of virtue is the striving to preserve oneself (IVp22cor). The more a person succeeds in obtaining his advantage and preserving his being, the greater is his virtue (IVp20). "Acting absolutely from virtue is nothing else in us but acting, living, and preserving our being (these three signify the same thing) by the guidance of reason, from the foundation of seeking one's own advantage" (IVp24).

Spinoza's version of egoism, however, is an enlightened one. Reason discerns that we need other human beings in order to survive and flourish. "To man . . . there is nothing more useful than man," and the more one human being flourishes, the more useful she is to others (IVp18; p35cor2). Reason thus guides us to seek the same good for others that we seek for ourselves, to be "just honest, and honorable" and to form bonds based on mutual trust and love (friendship), to submit to the common laws of the state, and to return hatred with love (IVp18sch; p46, p71,p73). The egoistic principle that everyone should seek his own advantage is the foundation not of immorality, but of morality and virtue (in the ordinary as well as Spinoza's sense of that term—IVp18sch).

Even though Spinoza's egoism is enlightened, there are two features of his doctrine which are difficult to reconcile with egoism. One is his assertion in IVp72 that "A free man always acts honestly, not deceptively." This proposition is puzzling because (1) the free man is the person who always acts according to reason; (2) reason for each person prescribes that he do whatever is conducive to his self-preservation; and (3) situations may very well arise in which a person can preserve his being only by deception. That Spinoza meant what he said in this propostion is shown by his remarks in the scholium which follows it. There he poses the question "What if a man could save himself from the present danger of death by treachery? Would not the principle of preserving his own being recommend, without qualification, that he be treacherous? His answer is negative. Spinoza's remarks in IVp72 and its scholium are problematic in light of his egoism because while an egoist—and particularly an enlightened egoist—may recognizes that there are limits on what she "should" do, those limits are a function of self-interest. Spinoza's remarks here, however, clearly state that deceptive or treacherous action is always prohibited by reason, even when not to act deceptively or treacherously means imminent death.

The second difficulty for Spinoza's egoism is his claim in IVp35 that "Only insofar as men live according to the guidance of reason, must they always agree in nature." Since he has already established that "Insofar as a thing agrees with our nature, it is necessarily good" (IVp31), it follows that insofar as human beings live according to the guidance of reason, what they do must always be good for one another. But reason counsels each individual to do what is most advantageous to her, hence, the true interests of everyone must always coincide.[2]

The line of thought which is generally taken to underlie Spinoza's presumption that the true interests of all persons coincide is as follows. Everyone needs the security and protection of an organized society in order to pursue or enjoy any good, and whatever else a person may seek, an organized society also provides the positive benefits of division of labor and the easy and efficient exchange of goods. Hence, all persons share a common interest in doing whatever is necessary to promote the existence of an organized society. In addition, since true human good consists in the perfection of the intellect, it is by nature something which human beings need not compete for, but which all can equally possess (IVp36). Finally, nothing can assist a person more in the attainment of this good than other human beings, especially those who are guided by reason (those who are already in possession of this good).

On this view the welfare of others is instrumentally linked with that of each individual. From this view it is supposed to follow that what profits one, profits everyone, and vice versa; and as Spinoza asserts in IVp35cor2, "When each man most seeks his own advantage for himself, then men are most useful to one another."

There is a problem with the "instrumentalist" line of thought. While it is sufficient to show that the true interests of all persons generally coincide, or coincide to some degree, it is not sufficient to show that they must always coincide, as IVp35 implies. As C. D. Broad pointed out, even though the highest good is non-competitive, the lesser goods which are needed in order that one may enjoy it are not:

> Philosophers and scientists and artists need as much food, clothing, shelter, and warmth as anyone else. And they need considerably more leisure, and a long and expensive training. Now the supply of all these things is limited. Unless some people mainly devote themselves to producing such things, and thereby forfeit their own chance of any great intellectual or artistic development, it is certain that scientists and philosophers will not have the leisure or the training or the freedom from practical worries which are essential to their intellectual development and activity.[3]

In order to justify the contention that insofar as human beings live according to the guidance of reason, they *must always* agree in nature, or *must always* be good for one another, Spinoza needs another line of thought than the one outlined above. In fact, another appears to be operative in the demonstration of IVp35. There Spinoza appears to argue that when I judge something to be truly good for myself it follows that it is good for each human being, because whatever is truly good for an individual human being must be good for her *human* nature; and since all human beings share human nature in common, what is truly good for one is therefore good for all.

We have already seen that in order to propound a general ethical doctrine Spinoza must assume that all human beings share a common nature or at least are sufficiently similar that it makes sense to speak of a general human good and virtue. We need now to inquire what this human nature is. The question is complicated by his view that universal notions such as "man" are formed by the imagination and do not indicate any common property of things. But even if he took "man" to designate some real property common to all human beings, it is hard to see how this would help his argument. Each person would still be a separate instance of the universal human nature, and there doesn't seem to be any reason why one instance shouldn't flourish independently of other instances.

What Spinoza needs in order to reason from (1) When I do what is truly good for myself, I do what is good for human nature, to (2) when I do what is truly good for myself I do what is good for every other human being, is a stronger way of identifying the nature which all human beings have in common. That is, he needs a conception of human nature which does not have numerically distinct instances, but which is strictly numerically one in all human beings. One possibility is that he thought of it as the nature of a complex whole—humanity—and as something that human beings share in common in virtue of each one being part of this whole.

Consider the relation between a complex finite individual and its parts. What gives a complex finite individual the unity of a whole, distinguishing it from a mere collection of different individuals, is that a constant relation or set of relations is preserved among its parts. If a change occurs in one part which, by itself, would tend to destroy that relation, then if the individual is not to be destroyed, there must be an appropriate response or compensating change in the other parts. Thus a complex individual is necessarily characterized by a tendency to maintain its being, which is nothing more than the tendency of its parts to react to changes in one another so as to preserve the relations which constitute the unity of the whole. The parts can therefore be seen as at least partially governed by the tendency of the whole toward self-preservation. In this sense, the nature of the parts involves the nature of the whole, although the parts are not instances of the nature of the whole.

The human body exemplifies Spinoza's concept of a finite individual. Its parts are partially governed by laws of homeostasis such that when certain sorts of externally induced changes occur in one part, other balancing changes occur in others. The nature or essence of the body as a whole consists in its parts being related in this way. To say that something, e.g., the heart, is a part of the human body, is to say that it is partially governed by a set of laws whose overall tendency is to preserve the body as a whole. Thus, the nature of the heart is partially constituted by being governed by these laws. Since the same thing can be said of every part of the human body, Spinoza could have said that every part of the body possesses the nature of the whole in common with every other part. That is, every part of the body involves the nature of the body as a whole, but is not itself a distinct instance of that nature.

Analogously, if Spinoza held humanity as a whole to be a complex individual whose parts are individual human beings, then the human nature which all human beings have in common would simply be the nature of the complex individual, humanity. According to this conception each human being is partially governed by laws which constitute the nature of the whole—humanity. The individual's nature is partially constituted by that of the whole, just as the heart's nature is partially constituted by that of the body as a whole. This view does not deny that every human being is himself an individual. The distinction between part and whole is relative in that every thing is both a whole consisting of parts and a part of a greater whole. But just as hearts would not be hearts if they were not parts of human bodies, human beings would not be human if they were not each a part of humanity.

One objection to this interpretation is that it seems obviously contradicted by empirical fact.[4] There is no world-society, and even single societies appear to lack the unity which this view requires. The response to this is that humanity is a large, but finite, individual. Consequently, its unity is necessarily subject to the disrupting influences of external forces. In addition a description of a thing under certain circumstances is not a description of its nature. To describe the nature of a thing we must consider it apart from any environment, as if it were free. If humanity were free, i.e., not a part of nature, its unity would be perfect and evident. Individual human beings would be governed in all their interactions by a set of laws whose overall tendency would be to preserve humanity as a whole. They would be, from our point of view, perfectly moral. That human beings do cooperate in social organizations, that they have the concept of a universal morality, and that many of them strive to live according to universal moral laws is evidence of the unity of humanity. That a good deal of human interaction is not harmonious is evidence that humanity, as such, is weak and needs to strengthen itself.

Like the free man (IVp67-73), a free humanity is only hypothetical; it is an ideal which can be approached but never attained because humanity is necessarily a part of nature. Spinoza appears to have had this ideal in mind when he wrote

> Man. . . can wish for nothing more helpful to the preservation of his being than that all should so agree in all things that the Minds and Bodies of all would compose, as it were, one Mind and one Body; that all should strive together, as far as they can, to preserve their being; and that all, together, should seek for themselves the common advantage of all (IVp18).

The interest or advantage of humanity builds a limitation into Spinoza's otherwise egoistic ethics. Reason counsels each of us to pursue what is truly for our advantage, but it perceives that we are essentially— not merely instrumentally—linked with all other human beings, and that we cannot flourish at the expense of humanity as a whole. This explains why, insofar as human beings act from the guidance of reason, they must always agree in nature or be good for one another. The limitation which the interest of humanity places on what an individual should to do in pursuing her own interest thus enables Spinoza to avoid one criticism which is justly aimed at ordinary egoism, namely, that it provides no way of deciding interpersonal conflicts of interest, which is not relative to an individual. To return to Broad's example: if it is in the interest of humanity as a whole that certain people have the leisure to study and develop their intellectual and artistic talents, while others lack such leisure, then the former should have it while others lack it, and reason counsels us all that this is the way things should be. The limitation which the interest of humanity places on what we can do to preserve our being or pursue our own advantage also can explain Spinoza's reasoning behind the assertion that a free man would never act deceptively or treacherously, even to save himself from imminent death. He must have viewed such actions as always detrimental to humanity, hence never in an individual's true interest. (Why, or even if, deceptive or treacherous action is always detrimental to humanity, is another question.)

Let us now reconsider the question of how to characterize Spinoza's ethical doctrine. One writer has argued that it should not be regarded as a morality because it does not recognize the effects of one's actions on other sentient beings as directly relevant to questions of how one should act.[5] On the interpretation of human nature which I have presented here, this is not true. Because it belongs to the nature of each person to be a part of humanity, we are essentially, not merely instrumentally, linked with other human beings, and to determine what is truly to our own advantage, we must consider how our action affects humanity. Should we continue to call Spinoza's doctrine egoistic? His expression of it is egoistic, but insofar as all human beings are part of the single individual which is humanity, their welfare and advantage coincide, and the distinction between egoism and its chief alternative, utilitarianism (the ethical doctrine based on the welfare of all), collapses.

Summary

Spinoza's ethics is thoroughly naturalistic. A thing is said to be good insofar as it is advantageous to someone or satisfies her desire, and evil insofar as it is disadvantageous or thwarts her desire. Thus, "good" and "evil" do not denote qualities of things, but only how things affect us, and are in general relative to the individual.

Insofar as human beings are influenced by passion, nearly anything can be an object of desire, hence "good;" what is truly good is what satisfies those desires that spring from us insofar as we act—i.e., insofar as we have adequate ideas. But insofar as we have adequate ideas we seek nothing but to understand; so understanding is our ultimate good, and things which are conducive to understanding are good in relation to it (useful).

Because we are finite, embodied beings, it is inevitable that we suffer passions and stand in need of many things outside us. One part of ethical wisdom is knowing and satisfying the needs of the body, doing what will sustain and enhance its abilities to affect and be affected by other bodies, so that the mind will be better able to think and perceive. Another is understanding and managing the passions. Only reason can judge the true worth of an object of desire. And while the desires directly generated by reason itself are often too weak to counter those generated by the passions, we can exercise a kind of indirect control through cultivating passive affects that "agree with reason," such as fear of the consequences of excessive pleasure or desire. Understanding how certain passive affects "agree with reason" enables us to to turn what is in itself harmful into something useful for achieving our own aims.

Spinoza's interpersonal ethics is expressed in terms of egoism; the fundamental "dictate of reason" is that everyone should love himself, seek his own advantage, and strive to preserve his own being as far as he can. But there are two features of Spinoza's ethics which are difficult to reconcile with egoism. One is his assertion in IVp72 that reason would never counsel a person to act deceptively or treacherously; the other is the implication of IVp35, that insofar as human beings act from reason, there will be no conflicts of interest among them, but what they do will always be good for one another. One way to understand these claims is to interpret Spinoza as holding that all human beings are essentially part of the individual which is humanity; and that the welfare of humanity in effect places a limit on what an individual may do to preserve his being, thus providing a decision mechanism to resolve what would otherwise be irresoluble conflicts of interest among individuals.

Endnotes

---

[1] The material in this section was previously presented in Steinberg 1984.

[2] That there are no conflicts of interest between persons who act from reason is also expressed by Spinoza in IVp37sch2.

[3] Broad, 43.

[4] Rice offers other objections and another view of human nature.

[5] Frankena, 96 - 98.

6
Method

Spinoza's philosophical methodology differs from that of his predecessor Descartes in a number of salient ways. The first is his use of the geometric method of exposition employed in his major work, the *Ethics*. A second is that Spinoza does not view overcoming doubt as a fundamental task of philosophy, although he thinks his philosophy does overcome it; and doubt plays no methodological role for him as it does for Descartes. A third is that knowledge of the mind or self is not primary, or basic to all other knowledge. At first glance Cartesian methodology may appear vastly superior to that of Spinoza. The *Meditations* is highly accessible to the reader, while the *Ethics* is nearly impenetrable; skepticism needs to be refuted; and the *cogito* and other immediate data of consciousness surely provide the most secure foundation on which knowledge could rest.[1] In this chapter we shall explore the basis for these differences between Spinoza and Descartes, and try to gain a deeper understanding of Spinoza's methodology.

Spinoza's Rejection of Methodological Doubt[2]

The Role of Doubt in Descartes' Meditations

Both Descartes and Spinoza are rationalist philosophers insofar as both hold that the source of our knowledge of reality lies within the mind, and that reasoning, not observation of the world through sense experience, is the way we obtain knowledge. The American philosopher C. S. Peirce, dubbed the rationalists' method the *a priori* method, and wrote of it that

> It makes of inquiry something similar to the development of
> taste; but taste, unfortunately, is always more or less a matter
> of fashion, and accordingly metaphysicians have never come
> to any fixed agreement, but the pendulum has swung
> backward and forward between   a more material and a more
> spiritual philosophy, from the earliest times to the latest.[3]

Peirce himself advocated the scientific method, one which involves testing beliefs against reality by means of sense experience. Writing roughly 250 years before Peirce, Descartes acknowledged the fact of wide disagreement among metaphysicians. But he took experience to be part of the problem, not the solution. He might well have agreed with Peirce that metaphysicians (other than himself) are guided by taste, since according to him the diversity of their views is a result of differences in their experience ("example and custom"), combined with the fact that no one is born able to make full use of his reason. On Descartes' view everyone, including metaphysicians, comes to maturity with his mind clouded with prejudices and generally irrational opinions derived from his own experience of things, including the influence of teachers and, through their books, ancient writers.[4] What is needed, therefore, according to Descartes, is a method which will enable us to overcome our entrenched opinions based on sense experience and penetrate to the truth of things.

Descartes' *Meditations* is a kind of manual for a reader to perform this task. *Meditation* I presents three arguments to undermine trust in the senses--that the senses are occasionally unreliable, that there is no way to tell the difference between dreaming and reality, and that we might be the creation of an omnipotent God who deceives us with regard to everything. These arguments serve as an exercise to induce the reader's doubt regarding all her former, sense-derived opinions. With her mind thus prepared she is led in subsequent meditations to the discovery of those things which can only be perceived by the intellect--the real nature of her mind, the distinction between mind and body, the existence and nature of God and the nature of genuine certainty.   Doubt thus plays an integral role in what Descartes calls his "analytic" method of demonstration, which he characterized as showing

> the true way by means of which the thing in question was
> discovered methodically . . .so that if the reader is willing to
> follow it and give sufficient attention to all points, he will
> make the thing his own and understand it just as perfectly as if
> he had discovered it for himself.[5]

By contrast, what Descartes calls the "synthetic" method

> employs a long series of definitions, postulates, axioms, theorems and problems, so that if anyone denies one of the conclusions it can be shown at once that it is contained in what has gone before . . . . However, this method is not as satisfying as the method of analysis, nor does it engage the minds of those who are eager to learn, since it does not show how the thing in question was discovered.[6]

On Descartes view, it is the analytic, not the synthetic, method of demonstration which is most appropriate for the subject matter of metaphysics, because in metaphysics the greatest obstacle is "making our perception of the primary notions clear and distinct."

The arguments of *Meditation* I lead the meditator to the point where he is "compelled to admit that there is not one of my former beliefs about which a doubt may not properly be raised." But despite this realization he also admits that out of habit he continues to hold his former beliefs, and proposes to rid himself of them by intentionally regarding them as false "until the weight of preconceived opinion is counter-balanced and the distorting influence of habit no longer prevents my judgement from perceiving things correctly." Thus he resolves:

> I shall think that the sky, the air, the earth, colours, shapes, sounds and all external things are merely the delusions of dreams which he [a malicious demon] has devised to ensnare my judgement. I shall consider myself as not having hands or eyes, or flesh, or blood or senses, but as falsely believing that I have all these things.[7]

These passages show that the Cartesian withdrawal from the senses has two distinct stages: first, by means of the arguments against the reliability of what the senses tell us, the meditator comes to the realization that all of his formerly held opinions may be false. This realization by itself is not sufficient to eradicate belief in the old opinions, but it does motivate him to make the effort to regard all of his former opinions as false, in order to counterbalance his tendency to retain them. By this means, the second stage--genuine Cartesian suspension of judgment--is reached. The mind at this second stage assents neither to the old opinions nor to their denial.

Spinoza and Doubt

Spinoza showed in his *Descartes' "Principles of Philosophy"* that he was aware of the heuristic role of doubt in Descartes philosophy.[8] In addition he shared Descartes' view that opinions which derive from our use of the senses are liable to error and tend to interfere with our ability to grasp metaphysical notions and truth. An example of such an opinion, which on Spinoza's view is particularly troublesome, occurs in Ip15sch, where he traces the failure to apprehend that extension is an attribute of God, to the imaginative conception of extension (quantity) as divisible, composed of parts, and (hence) finite. Nevertheless, Spinoza cast his own major work in the synthetic or geometric mode, and nowhere in expounding his own philosophy did he recommend doubt as a means of freeing the mind from erroneous opinions derived from the senses and preparing it for the apprehension of metaphysical truth.

To understand why Spinoza rejected doubt as a methodological tool, we must examine more closely what doubt involves for him. In fact he has two notions of doubt which, in important ways, parallel the two stages of the Cartesian meditator's withdrawal from the senses. The first, which I shall call second-level or reflective doubt, consists in a person's perceiving that her idea of a thing is inadequate (IIp49sch). The other consists in vacillation between two conflicting ideas, e.g., between my friend's coming to see me tonight, and his not coming (IIIp17sch; IIp44sch). This type of doubt does not involve reflective thinking. The two types of doubt appear to be separable mental states which can and often do occur together, and whose separate occurrence will each tend to produce the other. Each can, however, occur in the absence of the other.

Spinoza's reflective doubt--the perception that one's idea of a thing is not adequate--is not merely analogous to, but is the state of mind of the meditator, with respect to all her former beliefs, in the first stage of the Cartesian procedure. And Spinoza must surely agree with Descartes here, that this kind of doubt is not by itself sufficient to eradicate belief. On the contrary, once we have studied the *Ethics*, we know that all our opinions regarding our immediate surroundings at any moment are based on inadequate ideas, hence subject to this kind of doubt; but we do not for this reason cease to believe them. We do not, for example, cease to believe there is furniture in the room we are occupying. Spinoza's first level doubt (vacillation) is not identical with the state of mind experienced by the meditator in the second stage of Descartes' procedure, but it is analogous to it in two respects. First, it is the state which exists when conflicting ideas counterbalance one another; second, it is incompatible with belief. That is, insofar as someone vacillates between the idea that p and an idea which excludes p, she cannot be described as either believing p or believing not-p.

Had Spinoza chosen to use or recommend the method of doubt as a means of enabling the mind to withdraw from the senses and free itself from those opinions which are a barrier to the apprehension of metaphysical truth, it is first-level doubt or vacillation which would be required. Although such a state is not identical with Cartesian suspension of judgment, it is equally a state of non-belief. Why then did Spinoza not recommend first level doubt regarding all our former opinions (derived as they are from imagination--hearsay and random experience) as a means of removing the barrier such opinions present to the apprehension of metaphysical truth?

The Cartesian process of doubt in the first *Meditation* culminates in a state in which the meditator suspends judgment regarding the existence of everything in the physical world, including her own body. The Spinozist analogue to this state would be one in which the mind vacillated between its ideas of things, including that of its own body, as existing, and ideas of them as non-existing. But given Spinoza's theory of imaginative perception, it is impossible for the mind to form an idea of its own body as non-existing; hence no one can achieve a state of vacillation or doubt with respect to the existence of her body.

In order to form an idea of its own body as non-existing, the mind must have an idea which excludes the existence of the body, i.e., an idea of a thing x, whose existence is incompatible with the existence of the body. In order to have such an idea, however, the mind must have the idea of a modification of the body which was caused by x.[9] Since, by hypothesis, the existence of x is incompatible with the existence of the body, there can be no such modification of the body, hence no idea of x. But this only shows that the mind cannot have an idea of an actually existing thing whose existence is incompatible with its body. What we need to know is: can the mind imagine an actually non-existent state of affairs whose existence would be incompatible with the existence of the body? Again, the answer seems to be no. To do so would involve having an idea of a bodily modification identical to one which would be caused by a state of affairs which is incompatible with the body's existence. Put simply we can say: the mind cannot have an idea which excludes the existence of the body because all its ideas are directly ideas of modifications of the body, and there is no such thing as the way the body would be affected by a state of affairs in which it did not exist. First-level doubt, or a state of genuine disbelief, regarding the existence of the body is impossible.

The Geometric Method and the Structure of Knowledge[10]

That it is impossible for us not to believe our body exists explains why Spinoza rejected doubt as a methodological tool and also why skepticism regarding the existence of the material world was not a real issue for him. But it does not explain why he chose to give a "synthetic" rather than "analytic" presentation of his philosophy; and it leaves unanswered a serious challenge to his system, viz., why should the reader accept its basic starting points? As a number of commentators have pointed out, the basic definitions and axioms are not self-evident; and we have already seen in connection with the questions raised by DeVries concerning the definition of God, that Spinoza's contemporaries did not find them so.[11] Spinoza could have forestalled this sort of objection had he been willing to expound his philosophy analytically, i.e., in a way which would enable the reader to follow the route of discovery of his first principles. (Of course for Spinoza this route would not be via doubt, or a withdrawal from the senses.)

Spinoza's failure to give an analytic demonstration of his philosophy is undoubtedly connected with his admitted inability to formulate a satisfactory method of discovery. His early *Treatise on the Emendation of the Intellect* breaks off in the midst of an attempt to do just this; and as late as 1675 he wrote in response to a correspondent's request for his "Method of rightly directing the reason in acquiring knowledge of unknown truths," that his views had not yet been "written out in due order."[12]

Why was formulating a method of discovery such a difficult, even impossible, task for Spinoza? One explanation lies in the way he came to view what may be called the *justificational structure* of knowledge. By the "justificational structure" of knowledge I am referring to a particular way in which things said to be known or believed depend on one another. There are different relations of dependence among our beliefs. For example a detective might come to believe that a certain person X committed the crime he was investigating because he believed (falsely) that persons of a certain type are inclined to criminal behavior and that X was a person of that type. His former belief causally depends on the latter two beliefs, but is not justified by them. A mathematician might believe a certain (unproven) theorem is true because he believes it is similar to another which he knows to be true. Again, the first belief is not justified by the second, although it causally depends on it. In order for the detective's belief that X committed the crime to be justified he must come to believe that there is genuine evidence (e.g., fingerprints) linking X with the crime; and in order for the mathematician's belief to be justified he must come to believe the steps in a proof of the theorem. Justification is a matter of a belief's being one which someone ought to hold or invest full confidence in; and the justificational structure of knowledge refers to the way the confidence merited by some beliefs depends on that merited by others. The example of the mathematician also shows that what leads to the discovery of a truth need not be what what justifies our believing it.

Speaking very broadly and ignoring many complexities of the topic, one may say there are two types of view regarding the justificational structure of knowledge. Descartes held what is called a *foundationalist* or *linear* view of justification; Spinoza, by contrast, held a *holistic* or *nonlinear* view. Understanding this feature of Spinoza's philosophy provides a key to understanding why he chose the synthetic or geometric method to expound his doctrine, why he never managed to formulate a satisfactory method of discovery, and clarifies the status of the definitions of the *Ethics*.

Descartes' Foundationalism

Descartes is a foundationalist with respect to the justification of knowledge. That is, according to him there is a class of things which are known, or of which we are certain, independent of our knowledge of anything else. This class includes, for each person, knowledge of his own existence and facts about his immediate states of consciousness. All other knowledge logically rests on, or is justified by virtue of, this basic knowledge. For example, in answer to the question "How do you know that a perfect being exists?" Descartes would reply that he knows this because he knows that he has within his consciousness the idea of such a perfect being. His certainty that a perfect being exists logically rests on (among other things) his certainty that he has in his mind the idea of a perfect being; but the certainty of the latter does not derive from any other knowledge. He is certain that he has the idea of a perfect being, or is justified in believing that he has such an idea, independently of his knowledge of anything else. In the *Meditations* Descartes uses the analytic method to lead the reader from the apprehension of facts about herself which are indubitable or certain apart from anything else, to the discovery of things beyond herself, via a series of justified steps. His analytic method is thus at once a method of discovery and a method of justification.

Spinoza's Non-linear View of Justification

The doctrine of the *Ethics* clearly holds knowledge to be foundational in one sense. We have adequate knowledge of a thing only insofar as our idea of it is derived from or caused by another idea in our mind of the cause of the thing. Consequently, all our adequate knowledge terminates in ideas of what is cause of itself--God or one of God's infinite attributes. But this causal foundationalism does not commit Spinoza to a foundationalist view regarding the justificational structure of knowledge. That is, he need not hold that the ideas which are required to be the causal basis of knowledge (ideas of things conceived through themselves) are also self-justifying or certain independently of all other ideas. And he need not hold that ideas which are required to be the causal basis of knowledge are the single source of whatever certainty or justification attaches to other ideas.

In the *Ethics* Spinoza's answer to the question "how can someone know certainly that he has ideas which agree with their objects," is that a person can know this because he has an adequate idea of his idea (IIp43 and sch). Let us consider what is involved in such reflective knowledge. We have an adequate idea or knowledge of a thing when our idea of it derives from our idea of its ultimate cause, and thus is an idea from which all the properties of the thing can be deduced.[13] Put more simply, adequate knowledge involves the explanation of why the thing exists and has the properties it has. Thus, adequate knowledge of an adequate idea A will involve the cause of A and will explain why A adequately represents its object. But the explanation of why an idea A is adequate in some mind (or in the human mind in general) will necessarily involve the nature of the mind and its relation to the rest of reality, or in other words, the conception of the mind as God's idea of an actually existing body. Spinoza provides an example of adequate knowledge of an adequate idea with IIp38, whose demonstration proves that and explains why the common notions are adequately conceived by the mind. This explanation is that since the "objects" of the common notions are equally in the part and in the whole of all things (bodies) their ideas will be adequate in God insofar as God has any idea, including that of the human body; and since the mind simply is God's idea of the human body, these ideas will be adequate in the mind. Adequate knowledge (an adequate idea) of an adequate idea therefore involves virtually the entire basic metaphysical system of the *Ethics*. But if this is so, then certainty (the adequate idea or knowledge of an adequate idea) is necessarily an holistic property, one which emerges at the level of reflective knowledge only insofar as a person has the entire basic metaphysical system. Thus, in the order of justification, neither the idea of the human mind nor that of God (or that of any of God's attributes) is basic or primary. Rather the certainty of any idea or knowledge consists in a person's having at the same time the system of knowledge within which that idea can be completely explained.

We are now able to answer the questions regarding Spinoza's methodology which have been raised in this section. First, since justification or certainty for Spinoza is nonlinear or holistic in the way we have explained, the certainty or justification of the definitions and axioms derives from their place within the systematic explanation of the whole of reality. And the geometric presentation, which exhibits the interconnectedness of the whole, is particularly well suited to exhibit their justification. Further, we should conclude that one reason why Spinoza chose the geometric method of demonstration was because it was the one which best exhibited the justification of his philosophical views.

We can see too why Spinoza was never able to formulate a method of discovery, and why he did not give an analytic demonstration of his philosophy. On a nonlinear conception of justification such as Spinoza's there are no independently justified bits of knowledge from which one can proceed to build up the system, no independently justified starting points of knowledge. Knowledge does not grow by proceeding from one thing, indubitable and certain in itself, to another, but rather by making explicit what is already implicitly contained in the system as it stands, or by revising the system--replacing some of its component beliefs with others. Such revisions are justified with respect to the system as a whole, i.e., to the extent that the revised system has greater explanatory power or coherence than the unrevised.

Knowledge as Power and the Geometric Method

On Spinoza's view knowledge and its pursuit are not, and cannot be, disinterested. That we come to hold the beliefs we do is not independent of our desires.

We saw in chapter 3 that for Spinoza belief or judgment is not a matter of the mind's affirming (by an act of will), what it perceives (by an act of the intellect). For him every idea involves an affirmation, and there is no affirmation in the mind except that which is involved in an idea. Not every idea, however, is a belief. To believe that I am not at home right now is to have the idea that I am at home and another, stronger, idea which excludes my being at home, e.g., that I am in my office. My idea that I am at home involves the affirmation that I am at home since every idea involves an affirmation, but it is not itself a belief. The best way to understand Spinoza's notion of belief is that belief is a prevailing idea; to believe that p is for one's idea that p to be stronger than any idea one has that excludes p (whose object is incompatible with p, as my being in my office right now is incompatible with my being at home).

That our imaginative beliefs are influenced by our desires and the affects of pleasure and pain which give rise to desire is evident. Thus because we desire to increase our power of acting (pleasure) and to prevent its decrease (pain), we tend to imagine, hence believe, things which increase it, and avoid imagining things which decrease it. This is why we readily believe good things about ourselves—that we are attractive, generous, objective in our judgments, etc. It might seem that we are able to be disinterested in matters which are of no concern to us, e.g., the distance between Paris and London. Not every imaginative idea is an affect, i.e., involves an increase or decrease in our power of acting (IIIpost1), hence not every imaginative judgment is directly influenced by our desire. No imaginative judgments, however, are immune to the indirect influence of our desire. My desire to believe good things about myself which generates and strengthens my belief in my own objectivity may in turn lend support to my belief regarding the distance between Paris and London, or to any other belief I have. In addition, by Spinoza's principle of association of ideas and affects, any idea can acquire affective force (IIIp15).

Our beliefs which are based on reason or adequate ideas are also not disinterested or formed and maintained independent of our desires. Adequate ideas are the active manifestation of our power or striving to persevere in our being. They derive their force or strength from us. We experience pleasure insofar as we are able to think adequately and structure our ideas according to the order of the intellect, since such adequate thinking is accompanied by the reflective consciousness of an increase in our power of acting. Hence we desire to do this, and the more we do it, the more we desire it. We have, in other words, an interest in maintaining the system of knowledge which is based on our adequate ideas. We are not impartial.

We have already seen that skepticism regarding the existence of one's body is impossible for human beings. But what about a slightly mitigated skeptical position, which holds that while there is no doubting that a material world exists, still there is no reason to think that we know anything about the nature of that world? We have also seen in the last section that Spinoza's answer to this skeptic is that we know we have knowledge of the nature of the material world because we have adequate knowledge of our knowledge. Besides an answer, however, Spinoza has a diagnosis of the cause of such skepticism. It results from weakness of mind. Such a mind is not determined from within, by its own adequate ideas, but from without, by external things, in a disorderly fashion. Thus it may seem to such a mind that anything can be anything, that God could have human attributes, that there can be an infinite fly.[14] Such a mind will also be most vulnerable to the illusions of sense, to ideological propaganda, and to the sway of the passive emotions. The "cure" or remedy is to empower the mind by strengthening its adequate ideas.

It may be that Spinoza's choice of the geometrical form to expound his system was partly intended to accomplish this practical aim. The *Ethics* gives the reader what she has probably not yet acquired "by fate," namely a systematic framework of adequate ideas into which all her thoughts and experiences can be integrated.[15] A person who assimilates this framework has more than theoretical knowledge. To the extent that we are able to arrange our ideas according to the order of the intellect, we act or determine what we do. Ideas are dynamic entities; the more a person's are related in a single system, the more they reinforce one another. The person is thereby strengthened, becoming less vulnerable both to every sort of external influence. The *Ethics* is thus a practical tool in our struggle to become more free, not merely by pointing the way, but by giving us the only effective means.

Summary

For Spinoza genuine doubt concerning the existence of one's body is humanly impossible. For this reason a Cartesian-style withdrawal from the senses is impossible, and doubt plays no role in his philosophical method. Overcoming doubt is also not something philosphers must (or can) do before anything else. Doubt (on any subject) is remedied by knowledge or adequate ideas.

Spinoza's use of the geometric or synthetic method of demonstration is at least partly explained by his holistic or nonlinear view regarding the justification of knowledge. Unlike Descartes, Spinoza rejects the view that there are bits of knowledge of which we can be certain independently of any other knowledge. This includes knowledge of our own mind and of those things explained in the definitions and axioms of the *Ethics*. The certainty of these, like that of any other knowledge, derives from their place in the entire system of our knowledge. Thus, Spinoza chose the geometric method of demonstration because it was best suited to exhibit the interconnectedness of the system and the (consequent) justification of his philosophical views. It is also a consequence of his holistic conception of justification that there can be no analytic presentation of his system in the Cartesian sense, i.e., none which proceeds along a route of discovery via a sequence of fully justified (certain) steps.

Finally, Spinoza's presentation of his philosophy in the geometric form was also probably motivated by the practical value of a powerful system of ideas.

* * * * *

In my Introduction I focused on three features of Spinoza's philosophy which contribute to its unity: substance monism, naturalism, and his use of the geometric form of exposition. In subsequent chapters I have tried to show how the substance monism is developed, how naturalism characterizes all of his doctrines about the universe and human beings, including ethics, and finally, to explain why he chose the geometrical form of exposition. There is, however, one doctrine of Spinoza's which I have not touched on, which is a particular problem from the point of view of the overall unity of his system. This is the doctrine of the eternity of the mind, expressed in *Ethics* Vp21-p42. This doctrine is problematic first of all because it appears to contradict Spinoza's view that mind and body are one and the same thing, conceived under different attributes, and the more general thesis of the identity of modes of different attributes. If, as Spinoza asserts in Vp23, "The human Mind cannot be absolutely destroyed with the Body, but something of it remains which is eternal," then how can mind and body be identical? A second problem is that the view of the mind as eternal seems inconsistent with his otherwise exceptionless naturalism.

This problem is one with which many commentators, including myself, have struggled, and I will not attempt to offer a solution here. But I wish to point out two things. First of all, Spinoza himself points out in *Ethics* Vp41 that none of his earlier doctrines regarding morality or how we should live depend on the doctrine of the eternity of the mind. This suggests that there may have been some question in his mind regarding this doctrine.

The second point is somewhat more complicated. Spinoza makes a connection in the latter portion of *Ethics* V between the eternal part of the mind and its capacity to have adequate ideas. Although I have not mentioned them, there are also problems in Spinoza'a account of adequate thinking. Briefly, they come down to his assertion that in adequate thinking the mind is able to act or be the complete cause of its own states. Given that the mind is a finite mode, which in turn is determined by another finite mode, and so on *ad infinitum*, this assertion is problematic. At one time I took his doctrine of the eternity of the mind to be a solution to the latter problem.[16] That is, I took him to have seen that the view of the mind as merely the idea of an actually existing body was unable to explain how adequate thinking was possible; and to be offering in *Ethics* V an amendment to the original theory of the mind. To make a long story short, I no longer am convinced that in order to account for adequate thinking, Spinoza needs an actual eternal part of the mind—whatever that may be. And I am hopeful that along with a solution to the problem concerning adequate thinking, an interpretation of the last part of the *Ethics* (Vp21-p42) can be found which will render it consistent with his metaphysics and his naturalism.

Endnotes

[1] "The *cogito*" refers to the thinking self's immediate consciousness of its own existence.

[2] The material in this section was presented in Steinberg 1993.

[3] Peirce, 241.

[4] *Discourse on the Method* II, CSM I, 117-19.

[5] "Author's Replies to the Second Set of Objections," CSM II, 110.

[6] "Author's Replies to the Second Set of Objections," CSM II, 111.

[7] *Meditation* I, CSM II, 14 - 15.

[8] *Descartes' "Principles of Philosophy," Part I,* Prolegomena, in Curley 1985, 231.

[9] See ch. 3, p. 37.

[10] The discussion in this section is partly based on Steinberg 1998.

[11] Above, p. 15. See also Bennett 1984, 16-25; Curley 1986, 152-58; Hampshire, 30; Kennington, 97-98; Walker, 50.

[12] Letters 59 and 60.

[13] See chapter 3, pp. 39 – 40.

[14] An example used by Spinoza in the *Treatise on the Emendation of the Intellect* 58 (Curley 1985, 27).

[15] See the *Treatise on the Emendation of the Intellect*, 44 (Curley 1985, 21).

[16] Steinberg 1981.

Bibliography

Works by Spinoza

The Collected Works of Spinoza. Ed. and trans. Edwin Curley. Vol. I. Princeton, N. J.: Princeton Univ. Press, 1985.
The Letters. Trans. Samuel Shirley. Intro. and notes. Steven Barbone, Lee Rice, and Jacob Adler. Indianapolis: Hackett, 1995.

Other Works

Anselm, Saint. *Proslogion. Anselm of Canterbury.* Vol. I. Trans. and ed. Jasper Hopkins and Herbert Richardson. Toronto: Edwin Mellen, 1975. 87 - 112.
Aristotle. *The Basic Works of Aristotle.* Ed. and intro. Richard McKeon. New York: Random House, 1941.
Bennett, Jonathan. *A Study of Spinoza's Ethics.* Indianapolis: Hackett, 1984.
---. "Spinoza's Monism: A Reply to Curley." Yovel 1991. 53 – 59.
Broad, C. D. *Five Types of Ethical Theory.* London: Routledge & Kegan Paul, 1930.
Charlton, William. "Spinoza's Monism." *The Philosophical Review. 90 (1981): 503 - 529.*
Colerus, John. *The Life of Benedict de Spinosa.* London, 1706. In Pollock, *Spinoza: His Life and Philosophy.* 409 – 443.
Curley, E. M. *Spinoza's Metaphysics: An Essay in Interpretation.* Cambridge, Mass.: Harvard Univ. Press, 1969.
---. "Spinoza's Geometric Method." *Studia Spinozana.* 2 (1986): 151-169.
---. *Behind the Geometrical Method.* Princeton, N. J.: Princeton Univ. Press, 1988.
---. "On Bennett's Interpretation of Spinoza's Monism." Yovel 1991. 35 - 51.
Delahunty, R. J. *Spinoza.* London: Routledge & Kegan Paul. 1985.
Della Rocca, Michael. "Spinoza's Argument for the Identity Theory." *The Philosophical Review* 102 (1993): 183 – 213.
---. *Representation and the Mind-Body Problem in Spinoza.* New York: Oxford Univ. Press, 1996.
Descartes, Rene. *The Philosophical Writings of Descartes.* Vols . I, II. Trans. John Cottingham, Robert Stoothoff, Dugald Murdoch. Cambridge: Cambridge Univ. Press, 1985.
Donagan, Alan. *Spinoza.* Chicago: Univ. of Chicago Press, 1988.
---. "Essence and the Distinction of Attributes in Spinoza's Metaphysics." Grene 1973. 164 – 181.
Frankena, William K. "Spinoza's 'New Morality': Notes on Book IV." Freeman and Mandelbaum, 1974. 85 – 100.
Freeman, Eugene and Maurice Mandelbaum, eds. *Spinoza: Essays in Interpretation.* LaSalle, Ill.: Open Court, 1974.
Grene, Marjorie, ed. *Spinoza.* Garden City, N.Y.: Doubleday-Anchor, 1973.

Gueroult, Martial. *Spinoza I: Dieu.* Paris: Aubier-Montaigne, 1968.

Hampshire, Stuart. *Spinoza.* Rev. ed. Baltimore: Penguin, 1962.

Joachim, Harold H. *A Study of the Ethics of Spinoza.* 1901. New York: Russell & Russell, 1964.

Kennington, Richard. "Analytic and Synthetic Methods in Spinoza's *Ethics.*" *The Philosophy of Baruch Spinoza.* Ed. Richard Kennington. Washington, D. C.: Catholic Univ. of America Press, 1980. 293 – 318.

Lloyd, Genevieve. *Part of Nature.* Ithaca, N. Y.: Cornell Univ. Press, 1990.

---. *Spinoza and the Ethics.* London: Routledge, 1996.

Matson, Wallace I. "Spinoza on Beliefs." Yovel 1994. 67 – 81.

Parmenides. *Fragments.* Trans. and intro. David Gallop. Toronto: Univ. of Toronto Press, 1984.

Peirce, Charles Sanders. "The Fixation of Belief." *Collected Papers of Charles Sanders Peirce.* Vol. 5: *Pragmatism and Pragmaticism.* Ed. Charles Hartshorne and Paul Weiss. Cambridge, Mass.: Harvard-Belknap, 1965. 223 - 247.

Pollock, Frederick. *Spinoza: His Life and Philosophy.* London, 1880. Wm. E. Brown Reprint Library.

Rice, Lee. "Tanquam Naturae Humanae Exemplar: Spinoza on Human Nature." *The Modern Schoolman* 68 (1991): 291 – 303.

Steinberg, Diane. "Spinoza's Theory of the Eternity of the Mind." *Canadian Journal of Philosophy* 11 (1981): 35 – 68.

---. "Spinoza's Ethical Doctrine and the Unity of Human Nature." *Journal of the History of Philosophy* 22 (1984): 303 – 324.

---. "Spinoza, Method, and Doubt." *History of Philosophy Quarterly* 10 (1993): 211 – 224.

---. "Method and the Structure of Knowledge in Spinoza." *Pacific Philosophical Quarterly* 79 (1998): 152 – 169.

Taylor, A. E. *Elements of Metaphysics.* 7th ed. London: Methuen, 1924.

Wilson, Margaret Dauler. *Descartes.* London: Routledge & kegan Paul, 1978.

Walker, Ralph C. S. *The Coherence Theory of Truth.* London: Routledge, 1989.

Wolf, A. Introduction. *Spinoza's Short Treatise on God Man & His Well-Being.* Trans. and ed. A. Wolf. 1910. New York: Russell & Russell, 1963.

---, trans. and ed. *The Oldest Biography of Spinoza.* 1927. Port Washington, N.Y.: Kennikat Press, 1970.

Wolfson, Harry Austryn. *The Philosophy of Spinoza.* 2 vols. 1934. Cleveland: World-Meridian, 1958.

Yovel, Yirmiyahu. *Spinoza and Other Heretics. Vol.I: The Marrano of Reason.* Princeton, N. J.: Princeton Univ. Press, 1989.

---, ed. *God and Nature: Spinoza's Metaphysics.* Papers presented at the First Jerusalem Conference at the Jerusalem Spinoza Institute of the Hebrew University of Jerusalem. Leiden: E. J. Brill, 1991.

---, ed. *Spinoza on Knowledge and the Human Mind.* Papers presented at the Second Jerusalem Conference at the Jerusalem Spinoza Institute of the Hebrew University of Jerusalem. Leiden: E. J. Brill, 1994.